D1058757

THE
DICTATORSHIP
OF
WOKE CAPITAL

THE
DICTATORSHIP OF
WOKE CAPITAL

HOW POLITICAL
CORRECTNESS
CAPTURED
BIG BUSINESS

Stephen R. Soukup

Encounter BOOKS

New York • London

First American edition published in 2021 by Encounter Books,
an activity of Encounter for Culture and Education, Inc.,
a nonprofit, tax exempt corporation.
Encounter Books website address: www.encounterbooks.com

Manufactured in the United States and printed on
acid-free paper. The paper used in this publication meets
the minimum requirements of ANSI/NISO Z39.48-1992
(R 1997) (*Permanence of Paper*).

FIRST AMERICAN EDITION

LIBRARY OF CONGRESS CATALOGING-IN-PUBLICATION DATA

Names: Soukup, Stephen R., 1970– author.
Title: The dictatorship of woke capital / by Stephen R. Soukup.
Description: First American edition. | New York : Encounter Books, 2021.
Includes bibliographical references and index.
Identifiers: LCCN 2020035578 (print) | LCCN 2020035579 (ebook)
ISBN 9781641771429 (hardcover) | ISBN 9781641771436 (ebook)
Subjects: LCSH: Economics—Political aspects—United States—21st century.
United States—Economic policy—2009-
Classification: LCC HC106.84 .S658 2021 (print) | LCC HC106.84 (ebook)
DDC 322/.30973—dc23
LC record available at https://lccn.loc.gov/2020035578
LC ebook record available at https://lccn.loc.gov/2020035579

Interior page design and typesetting by Bruce Leckie

CONTENTS

WHAT IS WOKE CAPITAL?

On March 24, 2020, the United States government, which Lincoln famously called "the last, best hope of Earth," officially launched a "partnership" with BlackRock, Inc., the world's largest money management firm. With the economy suddenly in shambles, crushed under the weight of the global coronavirus pandemic and associated "social distancing" measures, the Federal Reserve desperately needed help navigating uncharted territory and administering and managing its brand-new corporate bond programs. And in its hour of need, the Jerome Powell–led Fed turned to Larry Fink and BlackRock.

It was an interesting, if unsurprising, choice for the Fed. With more than $7 trillion in assets at the time, BlackRock was already the undisputed king of the financial services world. More to the point, over the several previous months, it had also become one of the world's largest and most powerful advocates of what Fink called "a fundamental reshaping of finance." If anyone could help the Fed and help the nation, then it would seem that Larry Fink was the man.

The interesting thing is that Fink made his declaration on "reshaping" finance several weeks *before* he was tapped by the Fed and *before* he met with President Donald Trump, who later called him one of "the smartest people" we, the nation, have working to fix all our problems. Even before the coronavirus cratered the stock market and the American economy, Fink was already busy finding ways to fix that which he saw as broken, which included a great deal more than the fallout from a mere virus. Fink planned to "reshape" finance not just to save the country, but to save the world as well.

You see, Larry Fink is a born-again "fundamentalist." He's not a fundamentalist in the sense that market observers and participants might expect, i.e., someone with a deep and abiding dedication to market fundamentals or company fundamentals. Rather, Larry Fink is a religious fanatic, a believer in search of the pure, fundamental practice of his faith. Or, at the very least, by the start of 2020 he had decided to play one on TV. Fink had been building to a public profession of his faith for several years, and in late January, even as COVID-19 was already ravaging Wuhan, China, he made it official in a letter to clients of his firm (and a concurrent letter to CEOs). "We believe," Fink professed, "that sustainability should be our new standard for investing."

In so doing, Fink not only expressed his own belief in the importance of "sustainability," but he also assuaged what he said were customers who had told him they were extremely worried about climate change. These customers had told him, apparently, that they worried not merely about the "physical risk associated with rising global temperatures" but about "how the global transition to a low-carbon economy could affect a company's long-term profitability" as well.[1] He heard their cries and responded as a fellow believer.

Conveniently enough, by embracing sustainability as *the* value by which investments should be measured, Fink also aligned himself with the "best and the brightest" in the worlds of economics and finance— the great global institutions, the United Nations, the World Bank, the International Monetary Fund, the self-identified "guardians" of the postwar global order. He aligned himself with the Federal Reserve, which had already begun investigating the process by which it could factor climate change into its lending practices. Perhaps most notably, he aligned himself specifically with the Fed chairman, Jerome Powell, who, twelve years earlier, had founded the Global Environment Fund, a private equity firm focused on sustainable energy and investments.

In short, Fink aligned himself with and placed himself at the forefront of the "ESG" movement, an investment trend focused on Environmental, Social, and Governance matters in assessing a company's long-term value. He placed himself in the position to be crowned king, not just of the financial services world but also of "woke capital," the top-down, antidemocratic means by which some of the most powerful and best-known men and women in American business are endeavoring to change capitalism, the securities markets, and the fundamental relationship between the state and its citizens—and to "save" the world.

When the histories of this era are written, 2019 will go down as the year of ESG—the year of planning for investment instability that, as it turns out, did nothing to limit investment instability. American investors alone plowed more than $20 billion into ESG funds in 2019, more than four times what they had invested in ESG the year before. ESG became the hottest, fastest-growing, and most conscience-allaying trend in the investment business.[2] Larry Fink told clients that "By the end of 2020, all active portfolios and advisory strategies will be fully ESG integrated."

And then he took over the Fed's portfolios on behalf of the American people.

ESG investments promise solutions to issues that otherwise seem intractable. Thus, they have become an attractive alternative to at least two types of investors.

The first of these is the investor who very much wants to make gobs and gobs of money but doesn't want to seem crass and greedy. He wants to be seen as "socially responsible," even as he earns an eight- or nine-figure salary and amasses a net worth in the billions—a kinder, gentler Gordon Gecko for the twenty-first century. Think here of Jamie Dimon, the CEO of BlackRock's competitor JPMorgan Chase. Dimon wants the Lord to make him chaste, but not yet. He mouths the words of the creed but doesn't quite believe them. To him, ESG is the means to an end. And that end is Jamie Dimon and his friends getting filthy rich.

The second type of investor is the utopian/religious fundamentalist, the kind of investor who believes that he can change the world and can make himself rich in the process, a happy coincidence. This investor is the modern-day Calvinist, someone who believes that his wealth and success are outward signs of his righteousness. Likewise, he believes that a company's "value" as an investment is an outward sign of its adherence to the precepts of sustainability. To mix metaphors, this is the investor who buys stock in the company that makes the ropes with which the capitalists will be hanged, specifically because it will be used to hang the capitalists—the *bad* capitalists, the *other* guys, not enlightened, devout guys like him.

This second type of investor believes that changing the world will require eliding politics as usual and circumventing the will of the people, as expressed through political means. Like so many other projects before it, saving the world—from fossil fuels, from the patriarchy, from homophobia and other intolerances, from *capitalism*—requires that the people be cut out of the process. The *canaille*, you see, is simply too uncivilized, too unsophisticated, too unaware of its real interests and needs to be expected to muster the will to make the changes necessary. So someone else has to make the changes for them. Once those changes have been made, and the masses see what their betters have given them, then—and only then—they will awaken from the slumber of cultural hegemony and understand what is truly good and just in the world.

The good news for the utopian investor is that he has learned that control of money, control of capital, is all that men as sophisticated, educated, and cultured as he need to make the changes they desire. Moreover, they can make these changes without having to upset anybody. Indeed, that is one of the chief appeals of their ESG faith. ESG promises the best of all possible worlds. Not only can it change our culture and our civilization without involving those who cling to said culture and civilization, but it can do so painlessly, seamlessly, and most important, profitably.

If the world's troubles are caused by man's shortsightedness, then they can be corrected by taking the longer view, a broader, more expansive view of what it means to be successful. Success can—and should, man is told—be measured in terms that might seem unnatural at first, but that can be justified as an appeal to his better nature and a boon to his long-term prospects for safety, security, and material happiness. It is true that eliminating the very notion of an event horizon in investing, and in business more generally, requires a new type of thinking, a new management style, and a new asset allocation strategy. But then, that's what the best and the brightest do, isn't it: change the existing reality to better suit their needs and the needs of the many?

Why, the utopian investor asks, should we measure the success of a company exclusively in terms of the number of smartphones it sells every quarter, multiplied by the cost of a smartphone, minus the costs associated with making and distributing those smartphones? Why shouldn't we define success to include our beliefs and our values? Why shouldn't we add another variable to the equation, one that measures the "footprint" associated with the manufacture and distribution of the smartphones? Why shouldn't we demand—given the power our control of capital grants us—that our values be reflected in the investment of that capital? Why shouldn't we insist that our values—religious in nature and unpopular in the voting booths—be the standard for participation in our system?

That, in a nutshell, is the ESG movement, the movement that Larry Fink—now the *de facto* asset manager of the United States government—professes to lead.

As fate would have it, 2019 was also the year of the "stakeholder," a secondary but nonetheless important player in the growth of "woke" capital. In 2019, stakeholders became all the rage among the intelligentsia and the business elite, who were suddenly concerned that shareholders were getting too much attention, while stakeholders were given short shrift.

Now, to clarify, it's not that stakeholders aren't important and wonderful. They are. When a business expends extra time and energy to consider its stakeholders—which is to say its employees, its customers, its community, and so on—that's a good thing. No one anywhere has ever objected to companies caring about their stakeholders. No one. Ever. Indeed, any business that wants to be *in* business more than a few months takes its stakeholders into account whenever it makes a decision about…well…anything.

And that's precisely the reason the stakeholder crowd is so transparent and its concerns so affected. The shareholder/stakeholder distinction is the very definition of a false dichotomy. Worse still, it's a false dichotomy based on a clear and willful falsehood, a Big Lie, if you will. Shareholders are stakeholders too, important ones. And in many cases, stakeholders are also shareholders. But that hasn't stopped the virtuous from signaling their apparent dedication to a form of capitalism purportedly concerned with one but not the other.

Those who expend time and energy advocating the stakeholder model tend to be less aggressively devoted to "woke capital" than those who profess the ESG and "sustainability" faith. There is considerable overlap, of course, but it's probably fair to say that many of those who prattle on about stakeholders are merely appropriating the language of the believers. They are more akin to the Augustinian investors noted above than to already-converted true believers like BlackRock and Larry Fink. Make us chaste, Lord, but not before you make us billionaires!

Given this, it should come as no surprise that one of the leaders of the stakeholder movement, one of its highest-profile public advocates, is the aforementioned Jamie Dimon. In August 2019, the Business Roundtable (BRT)—a nonprofit organization whose members are the CEOs of the largest corporations in the United States—issued a statement in which it declared that its members had agreed to be less focused on shareholders and more focused on stakeholders.[3] The chairman of the Roundtable—none other than Mr. Dimon—declared in a press release that "The American dream is alive, but fraying." He implied that only by redefining the purpose of a corporation can that dream be saved. "These modernized principles reflect the business community's unwavering commitment to continue to push for an economy that serves all Americans."[4]

That's nice, isn't it? Yay, capitalism! As Dimon's language reveals, however, this "redefinition of the purpose of the corporation"—which is what the BRT called its statement—is rather strange. For starters, "modernized" is a nonsense word. It means nothing. It is a marketing term with no real substance attached, akin to "new and improved," but without the implication that anything has been made newer or improved. As for the rest of it, that too is nonsensical. Why, pray tell, would anyone need to change anything in order to allow it to better describe its existing "unwavering commitment" and its desire to "continue" doing what it's already doing? It's almost as if the entire declaration was fabricated for the express purpose of appearing to do something while doing nothing at all.

And, of course, that's almost entirely what this was.

To be sure, some small part of the Business Roundtable's declaration was purposeful. Among other things, the statement provides corporate executives with some cover for those occasions when they may wish to defy shareholder demands. Matt Levine, the author of *Bloomberg Opinion*'s "Money Stuff" newsletter, suggested that "in practice most disputes over corporate governance are not between shareholders and employees or shareholders and polluted watersheds, but between shareholders and managers." Therefore, the BRT's purported change of heart should be seen less as the result of CEOs having "thought it over and decided that employees and the environment are getting a raw deal," and more as an overt declaration by corporate managers "that shareholders are annoying."[5]

As with all of the moves made by less religiously dedicated woke capitalists, this change in the definition of the purpose of a corporation was an intentional and intentionally self-centered act. Not only did it give corporate managers a new weapon in their battle with shareholders, but it also allowed them to signal their own virtues to the most problematic of these shareholders. By agreeing to change the public focus of their mission to "stakeholders," the members of the Business Roundtable hoped to give themselves more leeway to do as they please, to pursue their own interests and their own political predilections, and to be able to call it by a noble name: stakeholder capitalism! But they also hoped to get the activists to shut up and leave them alone. As annoying as shareholders may be, activist shareholders are infinitely worse. And by acknowledging the activists' demands, the CEOs of the BRT hoped to satiate them, at least for a while.

But as some of those CEOs have already learned, and as the others will learn in time, that's not the way it works. Activist shareholders—most of whom pursue politicized ends and care less about a company's profitability and more about its alignment with their political posturing—are like sharks. They live to feed, not the other way around. They are always circling, always on the hunt for their next prey, their next tasty morsel. Worse still, they can smell the smallest drop of blood from hundreds of miles away, so any sign of weakness is interpreted as an invitation to attack and whip up a frenzy. By redefining the corporation to sound more ESG-friendly and appear more "sustainable," the Roundtable and its members simply chummed the water, exciting the advocates of woke capital and advancing the cause of those who would overtly politicize American business.

The good news is that 2019 was also a year of awakening. In 2019, after years of flying under the radar and, as a result, having a free hand to change American business to suit their own needs, the activists of woke capital pushed too far and alerted too many Americans, previously blissfully unaware, that a concerted effort was being made to undermine the last of the great institutions of the West.

On June 19, Tom Cotton, the Republican junior senator from Arkansas, took to the floor of the Senate to decry political activism on the part of American businesses. According to Cotton, "liberal" CEOs were using their companies to attack and undermine the will of the

American people in various localities around the country, and he, for one, had had enough of it.

"[T]his is a democracy," the senator intoned, "so not everyone agrees.... We resolve our differences and reach compromises through democratic debate. What should never happen is billion-dollar corporations trying to dictate these moral questions to us."

What had caught the senator's attention—and raised his ire—was a concerted effort on the part of several multibillion-dollar companies trying to do just that: dictate moral matters to the American people. Specifically, several large media companies—"Disney, Netflix, and Warner Media"—had begun a campaign to punish the people of Georgia by crippling the state's economy. Why? Because the elected representatives of the people had passed a law—in keeping with the values and beliefs of the state's residents—to restrict abortion after a fetal heartbeat could be detected. These mega-media corporations were unhappy with the law, so they were threatening to pull production of their projects from the state. It was blackmail pure and simple. Pulling business from Georgia would serve only to hurt Georgians, including, of course, many women. But the media companies had their principles—or had, more likely, been told by activist employees and shareholders what their positions should be—and they were determined to make a stand, a blatantly undemocratic and coercive stand.

As Senator Cotton also noted, about the same time, the CEOs of "hundreds of companies" signed a full-page ad in the *New York Times*, insisting that abortion restrictions like the ones enacted in Georgia were "bad for business." How, Cotton wondered, could protecting the lives of future customers possibly be bad for business?

Cotton complained that "as liberal activists have lost control of the judiciary, they have turned to a different hub of power to impose their views on the rest of the country." He was right, of course, and he succinctly identified the entire point of shareholder activism. But he didn't know the half of it.

What Cotton had stumbled upon was the burgeoning "dictatorship of woke capital," the title that the editors of *First Things* gave his righteous speech from the Senate floor. He had stumbled upon the outward signs of the ESG movement and the soon-to-be-unveiled "redefinition of the purpose of a corporation." In short, he had stumbled upon the effort of the political Left to harness the power of business, and especially capital markets, to advance overtly and exclusively political ends. There is no plausible fiduciary reason to claim that abortion restrictions/protection for the unborn is "bad for business." That was simply the language that the activists, the corporate executives, and their PR specialists had decided would allow them to play the victim and demand that democratically elected legislatures and governors change the democratically approved legislation that they had enacted. It was mere cover—and poor cover at that.

The problem was that the woke capitalists lost their temper. And when they did, they forgot what they were doing and why they had previously been doing it so surreptitiously. They forgot that their effort was supposed to be carried out stealthily, without raising the ire of the likes of Senator Cotton and without attracting the attention of Americans who did not share their beliefs about abortion. They forgot that most Americans are willing to accept and, frankly, ignore high-minded vagaries about "sustainability" and favoring "stakeholders" over pure profit, but are unwilling to ignore solid, concrete attacks on their personal beliefs and their right to advocate for them in the public square. For the first time in a long time, the woke capitalists found themselves confronted with a popular movement that was not just willing but also able to cut to the heart of their positive-rights–laden ethos. And in response, they overstepped, awakening a nascent but nonetheless furious resistance. They blew their cover and, in the process, revealed the dark underbelly of their effort to transform American business precisely as they had transformed every other institution of Western culture.

Senator Cotton was not the only party to take notice of the previously stealthy effort to politicize American business and use its power to advance an otherwise unpopular political agenda. Others in Washington took notice too, from Capitol Hill, down Pennsylvania Avenue to the White House, and then back over to 100 F Street Northeast, the headquarters of the Securities and Exchange Commission (SEC). The SEC was already aware of the concerns that Senator Cotton and others had raised, having followed the ESG investment movement since its inception and being acutely aware that the movement had its detractors in addition to its many ardent and aggressive fans.

Among the critics of the ESG movement and its effects on business and capital markets was a small, loose coalition of policy-oriented think tanks and other nonprofit operations that were keenly aware of the effort to undermine and politicize American business. They had been following the movement at least as long as the SEC had, and what they had discovered was a vast web of organizations, some religious, some political, some investment-oriented, but all dedicated to the same purpose: to use the structure of the capital markets to supersede the democratic will of the people to advance progressive policies that would otherwise be politically untenable. The coalition of organizations aligned against this effort saw the threat and structured their operations to push back, but found themselves screaming into the void.

While those on the offensive against American business were legion and were exceptionally well funded, those playing defense were few and far between and had a difficult time convincing anyone, especially the most fervent defenders of the markets, to pay attention. Market advocates, you see, are just that: believers in markets as efficient, self-correcting forces that compensate for and adjust to any external interventions. Who are you, they wondered, to stick your nose in from the outside and to try to "intervene" in the very forces that make capitalism work? Have faith, they preached. Let the markets handle their own business—as they always do.

But therein lay the rub. The markets weren't handling their own business, *couldn't* handle their own business because of the size and scope of the effort to undermine them. The forces arrayed against free and fair capital markets had grown so vast and so powerful, and had infiltrated so much of the structure of the financial services industry, that markets were clearly unable to self-correct. The intervention against free and fair markets was so advanced and so entrenched that it had become like Carl Sandberg's onion: every time you peel off a layer, you discover another layer underneath, and another underneath that, and then another still. The only hope was to enlist enough hands in the coalition to peel the onion quickly with as few tears as possible.

By attempting to undermine the will of the people in Georgia, the woke capitalists brazenly and arrogantly wielded their influence over American business and attempted to extend that influence in pursuit of more and more overtly political ends. They failed, however—at least to this point—to alter Georgia's abortion policy. Moreover, the flagrance of their disregard for the democratic process set off alarm bells throughout the political and financial services worlds, alerting the previously unaware of the impending danger. The woke capitalists overstepped. The war they had been fighting surreptitiously for years was exposed, and the battle, in turn, was joined.

CHAPTER 1

TO WHOM DOES WALL STREET BELONG?

For most of the last century, the mainstream and entertainment media have caricatured Republicans and conservatives as wealthy, uncaring, and completely out of touch with the average man. Daddy Warbucks—the original cartoon version, not the Hollywood reimagining—was an advocate of free markets and self-sufficiency. As such, he was opposed to welfare and the New Deal. This made sense, of course, in Depression-era politics; after all, Wall Street and its Republican allies had *caused* the Great Depression. After the 1928 election, Republicans controlled all the levers of power in Washington, so when the markets crashed just nine months into Herbert Hoover's presidency, he and his party bore all of the blame. When the Dow closed on July 8, 1932, it had nearly completely collapsed from its pre-crash highs. From the pre-crash peak to that post-crash trough, the Dow lost a staggering 89 percent of its value.[1] The depth of this plunge was so overwhelming and erased so much wealth that massive economic hardship followed inevitably in its wake. The subsequent series of cascading economic calamities were known collectively as the Great Depression. The financial and economic causes of the Depression were numerous and complicated, but the political causes were much less so. Wall Street and Republicans had overseen the carnage. And Wall Street and Republicans would suffer the political consequences.

By contrast to Hoover, Franklin Delano Roosevelt, the Democratic governor of New York, was heralded as a savior, the only man who could harness the power of the state to make everyone and everything whole again. Hoover, who in 1928 had won 444 Electoral College votes in a massive landslide victory against Alfred E. Smith, could only muster 59 Electoral College votes four years later. Republicans were swept from power in both houses of Congress as well, as Roosevelt and his "Brain Trust" promised to rescue those who had been beaten and battered by the Republicans, Wall Street, and the Depression they had caused. Though a patrician himself, Roosevelt connected with the people on a populist level, earning their complete and undying faith. As the great country music songwriter Bob McDill later put it in his "Song of the South," which became a smash hit for the band Alabama:

> Well somebody told us Wall Street fell
> But we were so poor that we couldn't tell
> Cotton was short and the weeds were tall
> But Mr. Roosevelt's a gonna save us all [2]

Wall Street, "fat cats," "country-clubbers," and "business tycoons" all became foils for the populists and even mainstream Democrats. Republican sociopaths cared about nothing other than their own wealth and power and were forever trying to take things from the poor, or trying to manipulate the downtrodden, or trying to cut government services for single mothers. By the 1980s, this caricature had become firmly ensconced in the public's imagination. Gordon Gekko was, of course, a fictional character, but to many in the country, and especially in Hollywood and the media, he was the embodiment of the Republican ethos. Greed is good, Gekko proclaimed, and the Reagan-era media promptly forgot that he and his proclamation were the figments of the overly active imagination of a Leftist film director named Oliver Stone. The decade of tax cuts, unparalleled economic growth, and the defeat of the Soviet alternative to capitalism was itself caricatured as "the decade of greed."

When Bill Clinton challenged George H.W. Bush for the presidency in 1992, the young Southern populist framed the campaign as a choice pitting the "out-of-touch" country-clubber and holdover from the decade of greed against the humble son of a single mother and champion of the middle class. Between Vice President Dan Quayle, who had risen to the heights of American power despite being unable to spell "potato," and

President Bush, who was so clueless that he was amazed by barcode scanners at the grocery store, Clinton's sophisticated campaign team painted a picture of an administration and a party far removed and insulated from the day-to-day lives of most Americans. "It's the economy, stupid," the Clinton team taunted Bush and Quayle, two men who, they insisted, owed their places in the world exclusively to their privilege.

Of course, it didn't matter to the Clintons and their entourage that the grocery-store scanner bit was a total fabrication[3] or that Dan Quayle's "potatoe" incident was considerably more nuanced than the media allowed.[4] All that mattered was that both incidents fit the stereotype of the rich, pampered Republican. And both, therefore, "proved" the need to take the country back for the "regular folks."

Very few in the media noticed, or if they did notice very few of them cared, that once he had beaten George Bush, Bill Clinton himself turned immediately to Wall Street for help formulating an economic plan. Robert Rubin, the former co-chairman and co-CEO of the Wall Street behemoth Goldman Sachs, became one of Clinton's most trusted economic aides, the director of his National Economic Council, and one of the most prominent and consequential economic players in decades. Rubin was sworn in as the secretary of the treasury on January 11, 1995, just in the nick of time to rescue his old friends and colleagues at Goldman from the consequences of their own recklessness in the Mexican Peso Crisis. In 1997, at Rubin's constant urging, President Clinton signed the repeal of the Glass-Steagall Act, a move that had been high on Wall Street's wish list for years. When Rubin left the Clinton White House in 1999, he returned to Wall Street and to Citigroup, where he proceeded to "earn" a staggering $126 million over the next ten years, thanks in part to the policies he pushed Clinton to enact.

In truth, the link between the Republican Party and Wall Street had always been a myth, a caricature from the Depression era that was false even then. Herbert Lehman, a liberal Democrat and a partner in his family's now-defunct investment firm, Lehman Brothers, had succeeded FDR as the governor of New York and later served in the Roosevelt administration. Investment banker C. Douglas Dillon served both the Kennedy and Johnson administrations as treasury secretary. And his replacement, Henry Fowler, left government service and became a partner at Goldman Sachs.

From the perspective of Wall Street, the thing that made the Clinton presidency so important, aside from Rubin's influence, was that it coincided with the American awakening to the importance of the mechanics of the equities markets. The Revenue Act of 1978 had created a tax loophole—Section 401(k)—that was intended to allow corporate executives to defer pay and bonuses without incurring immediate tax liabilities. In 1981 Ted Benna, a benefits consultant with the Johnson Companies, had the brilliant idea to allow employees to defer a portion of their own salaries the same way, creating a retirement savings vehicle that would complement traditional pension plans. By 1983, companies across the country were offering employees 401(k) savings plans. By 1990, 401(k) plans held some $384 billion in assets, and by 1996 that number had nearly tripled to more than $1 trillion.[5] From Clinton's inauguration in 1993 to the pre-crash market highs in December 1999, the Dow Jones Industrial Average nearly tripled as well.[6]

During the 1990s, Wall Street became democratized—and Democratized—which is to say that it became not only a savings option and object of economic obsession for the masses, but also a bastion of "progressive" political thinking.

Although the decade began with the election of a Southern Democrat, that Southern Democrat was different from his predecessors. He was also a Baby Boomer, the first of his generation elected president. And he brought with him the Baby Boomer moral ethos, which is to say their relaxed attitudes toward sex, about marriage, about religion, faith, and family. Bill Clinton would be the last of the Southern Democrats who could win an election with much support from the old South. Eight years later his vice president, Al Gore, the pride of Tennessee, couldn't carry his home state in his loss to George W. Bush. If he had, he, not Bush, would have been the forty-third president. But by the time he ran, after eight years as Clinton's second-in-command, the cultural and political landscape had shifted beneath his feet. The realignment that had begun with the Baby Boomers' cultural awakening in the 1960s was complete.

And it wasn't only the South that shifted its alliance. The parties essentially swapped places on the electoral map, with the Republicans taking control of the new Solid South and the Democrats owning both coasts, including, most notably, Manhattan's Financial District. Over a span of sixteen years, from 1992 to 2008, Wall Street shifted aggressively to the left.

Goldman Sachs co-CEO Jon Corzine served in an advisory capacity to the Clinton administration and, after heeding the New York Fed's call to arrange a bailout of Long-Term Capital Management, got the itch to play politician, eventually serving as both a Democratic senator from New Jersey and the governor of the state. And while the old South may have let Al Gore down, Wall Street picked him right back up again. In 2004, with the assistance of David Blood, the former CEO of Goldman Sachs Asset Management, Gore founded Generation Investment Management, a "sustainable" asset management firm and one of the first big players in the ESG investment space.

By the time the 2008 election cycle rolled around, Wall Streeters had fully and firmly embraced the Democratic Party and actually dragged it leftward. Hillary Clinton, then the sitting senator from New York, was pushed aside by her adopted home state's most affluent and influential residents in favor of Barack Obama, the young, charismatic, ideological *tabula rasa* from Illinois. Wall Street loved Obama and especially loved his social liberalism and his economic malleability.

During the 2006–2008 election cycle, Wall Street ponied up big for the Democrats and especially for Obama. Goldman Sachs (its PAC, its employees, and their immediate families) was the second-largest donor to Obama overall. J.P. Morgan was fifth, Citigroup seventh, and Morgan Stanley rounded out the Top 20.[7] The Democratic takeover of Wall Street was complete.

In a long post-election piece for *National Review*, Kevin Williamson noted that the Republicans had "lost Gordon Gekko," their erstwhile indefatigable caricature.[8] Williamson also explained, in large part, how the loss had thoroughly changed the face of Wall Street. He quoted one bond trader who told him, "Of course these guys aren't conservative. Why the [expletive deleted] would they be? We're talking about guys who live in Manhattan, guys with manicures and eight-figure bank balances. And their wives—their wives aren't showing up at parents' day at Brearley with a Sarah Palin button. It'd be like showing up in flip-flops from Walmart. Like showing up in a [rather lengthier expletive deleted] tracksuit."

The differences between Wall Street in 1988 and Wall Street in 2008 were shocking. The transformation was nothing less than total. In the

1980s, Republicans in pop culture looked like Randolph and Mortimer Duke, the wealthy commodity brokers in the movie *Trading Places* who toyed with people's lives just for fun. By the 2010s, however, Republicans were much more likely to be compared to Bo and Luke Duke, the reckless, redneck country boys who drove gas-guzzling cars and clung bitterly to their God and their guns.

The question is how that transformation took place, what changed over two decades to push good ol' country boys from Left to Right and wealthy Wall Streeters from Right to Left.

The simple answer is that the traditional Left died. And while the news of its death had not yet been relayed to all four corners of the earth by 1988, it most certainly had by 2008. This death of the traditional Left was not sudden. It suffered slowly, agonizingly for decades, starting at the end of World War I.

Among other things, the traditional Left promised that which could not be delivered. Rousseau's embrace of the "egalitarian State of Nature" enabled and encouraged a second, quasi-secular, post-Christian outbreak of revolutionary, chiliastic fantasies throughout the West. But like all such fantasies, these were inevitably doomed to fail, and this failure carried consequences.

In the West, the failure of the Left to deliver on its promised Utopia exacerbated a crisis of belief and elevated the epistemological skepticism of Nietzsche to new heights. In response to socialism's disappointments, the Left abandoned reason, abandoned "reality," and, in the end, rejected the Enlightenment itself in favor of relativism.

All of this constituted a death blow for the Left as it had existed. The Left was, after all, specifically and incontrovertibly a product of the Enlightenment. In fact, its sole purpose was to advance the so-called "Enlightenment Project," which turned into a three century–long attempt to construct a reason-based moral system to replace the Judeo-Christian framework.

This project, however, was doomed from the beginning by its refusal to recognize the premise upon which the Christian moral system was based: that man is flawed and neither reason nor science could fix him. Man could not—and *cannot*—be perfected. His "Millennium," which is to say his "paradise," is otherworldly. It is beyond that which he, with his imperfect nature, is able to create on Earth.

But while the quest for a better system failed, it nevertheless managed to damage Christianity so badly that by 1884, Nietzsche was able to declare that God was dead. Ironically, but unsurprisingly, this "victory" on the part of the Left created the conditions for its own demise. The movement drew its nourishment from its hatred of Christianity, which it claimed was responsible for all of mankind's woes. Naturally, then, as Christianity lost its previously unrivaled importance, the Left did as well.

The failure of the Left to deliver its promised pseudo-Christian Utopia created a crisis of confidence and, in turn, a crisis of reality. The American liberal dream managed to struggle along for its first few decades, but by the 1960s it was evident that the narrow economic successes that state liberalism enjoyed were driven primarily by noneconomic, non-repeatable events, such as the flight of gold from pre-war Europe, the war effort itself, the post-war American geopolitical hegemony, and the post-war demographic boom. The comparative normalcy of the 1960s and the 1970s more or less ended the Keynesian fantasy.

But if the American Left's failures were spectacular, the global Left's failures were more spectacular still. The viciousness and murderousness of Stalin's purges, the cold-blooded slaughter of millions of Chinese peasants, the violence, the bloodshed, and most especially the economic failure of the world's Leftist regimes belied the blissful idealism of the Marxist dream.

This book is divided into two sections. The first of these provides a brief history of the evolution of the Left from the economic ideology that spewed forth from Marx's poisoned pen to a cultural *weltanschauung* that denies the relevance and even the existence of its ideology's prior failures and appeals strictly to the vanity of the upper classes rather than the suffering of the working class. The second section documents the effects of this change on the capital markets and on business more generally, the damage done already and the damage yet to come.

The transformation of Wall Street was no accident. It was the product of a long, careful process, a march through various other institutions, turning them on their heads until the titans of "capitalism" had been fully convinced that their surrender to the culture was not merely inevitable but constituted the only morally legitimate path.

PART I

WELL, HOW DID WE GET HERE?

CHAPTER 2

WILSON, WALDO, AND THE FED

O ur story—the story of the politicization of business and of its
funding sources—has two starting points, two fountainheads
from which sprang streams that wound their way independently
through Western civilization for nearly one hundred years, converging
near the end of the last century to form a powerful river of political agita-
tion disguised as "good corporate governance." These two streams—the
streams of contemporary liberalism—are diametrically opposite each
other, one positing the belief that the entire world and all of man's social
behaviors can be analyzed through the lens of objective science and the
other insisting that this scientifically observed surface reality represents
the repression of man's true nature. And yet, somehow, they managed to
merge to form one massive, self-contradictory mess of moral, political,
and economic activism that serves only its own perceived interests.

In this sense, then, our story begins as all stories of misguided and
malicious politics in the West begin, with the Enlightenment. But for the
sake of practicality, we can reasonably skip the first one hundred–plus
years after this watershed and start our story in Baltimore, Maryland, in
1876.

Three years prior, a wealthy Quaker bachelor and railroad magnate
named Johns Hopkins died, leaving the enormous sum of $7 million
(the equivalent of roughly $150 million today) to found a hospital and
university. This university was to be like no other in the United States.
Whereas Harvard was founded to train Unitarian and Congregational

clergy, Yale was founded to teach theology and religious languages, Dartmouth was founded to teach Christianity to Native Americans, Princeton was founded to serve as a seminary for Presbyterian ministers, and so on, Johns Hopkins was founded not just to teach but to "discover" as well. Johns Hopkins was founded specifically and purposely to create or uncover new knowledge. In his inaugural address, Daniel Colt Gilman, the University's first president, declared that its mission would be "To educate its students and cultivate their capacity for lifelong learning, to foster independent and original research, and to bring the benefits of discovery to the world." Or, as Johns Hopkins University puts it today, its job is not to teach its students the knowledge *of* the world, but to uncover "knowledge for the world."[1]

Modeled after Germany's famed Heidelberg University, Johns Hopkins, in turn, became the model for the American research university more generally, an institution designed to produce new knowledge and to embrace "progress" as a defining value. In the physical sciences, this was and is both understandable and admirable. In the specific case of Johns Hopkins, the University's benefactor wanted the hospital to be on the cutting edge of medicine and for the medical college to train physicians capable of keeping it there. And, for the most part, that has been the case.

Unfortunately, at the time, the standard Western post-Enlightenment philosophical *weltanschauung* still clung to the notion that a "science of man" could be developed to mimic the natural sciences. David Hume conceived of himself as the "Newton of the mind," while Saint-Simone and Hegel both professed to discover the "science" of history. This "historicism," plus that which Friedrich Hayek later called "scientism," were the beliefs that human affairs were merely extensions of the physical sciences.

Historicism was the epistemological ethos of the German university during the nineteenth century, so it is no surprise that Hopkins, modeled on the finest such university, would be similarly enmeshed in this tradition. In 1881, Johns Hopkins hired a man named Richard Ely as a professor and director of its Department of Political Economy. Ely would prove to be the perfect "Hopkins man" and would forever change the ways in which Americans view politics, society, and especially economics. Though he was an American who earned his bachelor's degree at Columbia University, Ely took his PhD at Heidelberg, studying under

Karl Knies, a stalwart of the historical school. Ely was a great admirer of Gustav von Schmoller, the leader of the "younger" historical school of economics and, by extension, of Bismarck's state socialism. Ely returned to the United States a fully dedicated historicist and enthusiastic supporter of the Bismarckian welfare state.

Ely was also one of the most prominent and influential advocates of the "Social Gospel," a religious movement spawned by the Second Great Awakening, which posited that the state can and should be harnessed to fix the problems of society and to make man's existence more "Christlike." Ely believed that the state had a responsibility to fix all of man's societal problems, including, among others, poverty, alcoholism, crime, racial tensions, slums, and child labor. He believed, moreover, that the state should do all of this *in God's name*. Ely was guided in his beliefs about economics, religion, and the state by the complementary principles "God works through the states to carry out his purposes more universally than through any other institution" and "Christianity which is not practical is not Christianity at all."[2]

For various reasons, mostly pragmatic, Ely portrayed himself as an opponent of socialism, insisting that he believed firmly in the value of private property. Like Bismarck before him and countless others since, Ely believed he had found a "third way," one that made socialism unnecessary but that nevertheless guarded against the predations of laissez-faire economics and "plutocracy." He wrote that his "school" of economics does "not acknowledge laissez-faire as an excuse for doing nothing while people starve, nor allow the all-sufficiency of competition as a plea for grinding the poor," but rather "denotes a return to the grand principle of common sense and Christian precept." Therefore, he insisted, "Love, generosity, nobility of character, self-sacrifice, and all that is best and truest in our nature have their place in economic life."[3]

In all of this, Ely established himself as one of the leading voices of the new "progressivism" and also became the single most important figure in the transformation of the American state and the American sociopolitical mindset. The Americans whom Tocqueville observed believed that charity and good works are the responsibility of individuals, local communities, and civic organizations. The America that Richard Ely fashioned, by contrast, is one that sees the state as the natural and necessary "administrator" of these responsibilities. Whereas traditional

American Christianity advocated for voluntary community leavened by the principles of prudence and imperfectability, Ely demanded a "coercive philanthropy" that could be used to "establish among us true cities of God."[4] As Jonah Goldberg once noted, referencing Eric Voegelin's famous description of the Left's Gnostic tendencies, "More than any other thinker, Ely introduced the drive to immanentize the eschaton into the mainstream of progressive thinking…."[5]

Perhaps Ely's greatest influence, however, was that which he exerted on his students. And perhaps greatest among his students was a young PhD candidate at Johns Hopkins named Thomas Woodrow Wilson. Wilson would, of course, go on to become not just the twenty-eighth president of the United States, but the father of American public administration as well.

Wilson was, without question, a disciple of Ely's in every sense of the word, which is to say that he not only studied under the proto-progressive giant, absorbing his faith firsthand, but he also took that faith and proselytized it to the four corners of the earth. While Wilson was still a student, he and Ely began collaboration on a book that was to trace the history of "political economy" in the United States.[6] The book was never finished, but it was clear from his own notes that Wilson had very much absorbed Ely's understanding of "political economy" and his belief in the "scientific" nature of their undertaking.

In 1885, Ely, along with John Bates Clark and Henry Carter Adams, founded the American Economics Association. He did so after consultation with his student, Wilson, who was also elected to the Association's first governing council. In its statement of principles, the Association adopted a very clear and very Ely-esque approach to the field of economics. "We regard the state as an educational and ethical agency whose positive aid is an indispensable condition of human progress," the document declared, and "[we believe that] the conflict of labour and capital has brought to the front a vast number of social problems whose solution is impossible without the *united efforts of Church, State, and Science* [emphasis added]."[7] That last bit there is the key. The unification of faith, government, and "scientistic" methodologies would become the heart and the soul of much of the American Left for decades to come. This was Ely's vision, and it became Wilson's vision too—as well as his personal political mission.

If Richard Ely was the Millenarian prophet of American progressivism—and he was—then Woodrow Wilson was the trusty acolyte who followed behind and turned the prophet's ideas into reality. He was St. Paul to Ely's Jesus, or, more fittingly, Molotov to Ely's Stalin. Ely had the broad religiopolitical road map. Herbert Croly had the theoretical rationalization for undermining and upending the constitutional order. But Wilson was the man of action. Wilson formulated the plans by which the theology could be implemented and the constitutional order could be upended. In the first case, he would employ the idea that politics and administration should be separated from one another, with the "experts" handling the day-to-day chores of governance. And in the second, he would join Croly in attacking the Constitution and its relevance and then, once ensconced in power, would use the authority of his office to do real and permanent damage to the constitutional order, overseeing the creation of a new political and economic apparatus that dominates the "administration" of economic policy to this day.

Not long after completing his doctoral work at Johns Hopkins, Wilson penned the paper that would become his defining academic achievement. In 1887, the newly founded *Political Science Quarterly* published Wilson's "The Study of Administration," which earned him the title of "father of public administration." Wilson started the piece with the declaration that it "is the object of administrative study to discover, first, what government can properly and successfully do, and, secondly, how it can do these proper things with the utmost possible efficiency and at the least possible cost either of money or of energy." From there, he launched into a diatribe about the difficulties that face visionary reformers like him and Ely and what he saw as the dubiousness and the danger in the notion that ordinary people should be allowed to run their own lives in the complex modern world. As you read the following excerpt from Wilson's definitive article, note how the words practically drip with condescension for and loathing of the people:

> In government, as in virtue, the hardest of hard things is to make progress. Formerly the reason for this was that the single person who was sovereign was generally either selfish, ignorant, timid, or a fool, —albeit there was now and again one who was wise. Nowadays the reason is that the many, the people, who are sovereign have no single

ear which one can approach, and are selfish, ignorant, timid, stubborn, or foolish with the selfishnesses, the ignorances, the stubbornnesses, the timidities, or the follies of several thousand persons, —albeit there are hundreds who are wise. Once the advantage of the reformer was that the sovereign's mind had a definite locality, that it was contained in one man's head, and that consequently it could be gotten at; though it was his disadvantage that that mind learned only reluctantly or only in small quantities, or was under the influence of some one who let it learn only the wrong things. Now, on the contrary, the reformer is bewildered by the fact that the sovereign's mind has no definite locality, but is contained in a voting majority of several million heads; and embarrassed by the fact that the mind of this sovereign also is under the influence of favorites, who are none the less favorites in a good old-fashioned sense of the word because they are not persons but preconceived opinions; *i.e.*, prejudices which are not to be reasoned with because they are not the children of reason.[8]

Wilson is generally remembered by posterity as the "visionary" who proposed the League of Nations, which, revisionist historians insist, could have prevented World War II, had Henry Cabot Lodge not been so stubborn.[9] In truth, the League is but a bit player in Wilson's legacy and would have been, even if the United States had joined. Wilson's real legacy is tied to two developments that have had profound impacts on American society and especially the American understanding and application of capitalism.

The first of these, as noted above, is the founding of the American study of public administration. The notion of an appointed professional bureaucracy did not originate with Wilson, of course. Germany had established a professional bureaucratic apparatus roughly a century before. And the history of the Republican Party during and after Reconstruction is very much the story of a party torn apart by corruption and the need for civil service reform. In 1871 President Ulysses Grant created the United States Civil Service Commission, and twelve years later, President Chester Arthur signed the Pendleton Civil Service Reform Act, which was intended to end the Jacksonian "spoils system" and create a professional and merit-based bureaucracy.

Still, Wilson advanced the academic debate considerably. And his most notable contribution to this debate was one that would have a profound effect on the American public arena for more than a century. It also explains, in part, the effort on the part of some business leaders to advance their political agendas through nonpolitical means, that is, their businesses.

As is clear from the passage above, Wilson shared Ely's annoyance with and distaste for "the people." The irony of the Prairie Populists and Progressives placing their faith in an "elite" so thoroughly dedicated to removing the power to control their day-to-day lives from the masses and placing it in the hands of a small, specially educated, administrative gentry class is thick. Nevertheless, this is exactly what happened. And while Wilson played the role of dutiful democrat, he pushed ideas that would, essentially, emasculate democratically elected government. "The field of administration," he wrote, "is a field of business. It is removed from the hurry and strife of politics... administration lies outside the proper sphere of *politics*." Therefore, he continued, "Administrative questions are not political questions. Although politics sets the tasks for administration, it should not be suffered to manipulate its offices."[10]

Although he never used the phrase, and it didn't come into vogue until more than a half-century later, this prescription of Wilson's to separate administration from politics became known in public administration and policy circles as the "politics-administration-dichotomy." Wilson—like Ely, and Croly, and John Dewey, and the rest of the proto-Progressives—believed that the only way to handle the problems of society was to create a class of "professional" administrators, trained in the "science" of administration to manage society more rationally and carefully than the masses would, if left to their own devices.

Wilson's early entreaties to separate administration from politics were seconded by the legal scholar Frank Goodnow. Goodnow had studied law at Ely's alma mater, Columbia, and, like Ely, headed off to Germany to study at the University of Berlin. When he returned, Goodnow taught at Columbia for many years before becoming the third president of Johns Hopkins in 1914. His classic book *Politics and Administration: A Study in Government* was published in 1900 and helped place him among the leaders of the new "sciences" of politics and administration. Like Wilson, Goodnow rejected the merits of the American founding, arguing that the Founders' obsession with "private rights" had helped make Americans "a lawless people."[11] Most important, Goodnow, who would become the first president of the American Political Science Association, also echoed Wilson's call for the "scientific" training of government administrators, whose function should be separate and distinct from political influences.

Over the course of the first quarter of the twentieth century, Wilson's ideas, coupled with Goodnow's, were added to the management theories of Frederick Taylor to create the corpus of an intellectual and educational administrative "science." Leonard D. White codified this corpus into a basic curricular study guide with the publication of the first textbook in the field in 1926.[12] Thus the politics-administration dichotomy became a part of the official canon of public administration. Or, to put it more bluntly: the idea that the people are too ignorant and too selfish to vote for that which is in their own best interests, or the best interests of society as a whole, was established as a defining principle of American public management.

This basic consensus opinion of administrators' responsibilities held until well after World War II. In the late 1940s, however, the ground began to shift, and views on the politics-administration dichotomy began to change. The publication of Dwight Waldo's *The Administrative State* in 1948 heralded a definitive break with the Wilson-Goodnow consensus on the rigid separation of politics and administration. As one scholar put it, *The Administrative State* "established the alleged indefensibility of the politics-administration dichotomy, so that, for about half a century, the dichotomy has been treated like geocentrism in astronomy: Perhaps it was once believed in, but now we know better."[13]

There was a catch, however. Waldo's principal objection to the dichotomy was not based on a democratic or republican repulsion at the idea that the day-to-day function of government should be removed from the hands of the sovereign, which is to say the people. Rather, his objection was to the idea that administration could be "scientific." He argued that the distinction between decision and execution, which is how he conceptualized the dichotomy, was false. Waldo's view, which he termed "heterodoxy," was based on his belief that it was impossible, in the practice of administration, to distinguish between "value" and "fact." Rejecting the positivism of his contemporary Herbert Simon, Waldo concluded that both politics and administration were value-laden exercises and should be treated as such.

Empirically, it is clear that Waldo's assertions were correct, and that the process of administering the functions of government cannot be done in a purely "scientific" manner. In theory and practice, it requires the application of values. His contributions to the debate, however, were not interpreted as mere observations. They were, instead, taken as a license for administrators (and their educators) to become value *advocates*. In this sense, Waldo's contributions constitute a watershed in administrative/bureaucratic practice in the United States, a rejection of pure positivism and a slide toward a more enduring antipositivism. In isolation, such a slide could be seen as a minor development, a mere concession to reality. But, of course, Waldo's ideas were neither offered in isolation nor heeded in a vacuum. They took place against the backdrop of a cultural revolution of sorts, the "second stream" of American liberalism noted above and discussed below.

In 1968, Waldo hosted a very famous public administration conference that came to be known as "Minnowbrook" because it was held at the Minnowbrook Conference Center on the campus of Waldo's then-new employer, the Maxwell School of Citizenship and Public Affairs at Syracuse University. The conference was not only an enormous hit among educators, but it also took on legendary status among administrators—that is to say, public bureaucrats. In 2018, on the conference's fiftieth anniversary, the Maxwell School remembered the man and his contributions, noting that "Waldo's 1948 book challenged the idea that public administration is value-neutral, performed in a dispassionate, almost mechanical manner. He argued that *public servants should become active, informed, politically savvy agents of change*" [emphasis added]. George Frederickson, a public administration professor at the University of Kansas and the organizer of "Minnowbrook II" in 1988, told the Maxwell School magazine that Waldo's contributions included "three lasting themes in PA: social equity; democratic administration; and proactive, advocating, non-neutral public administration."[14]

By the start of the 1970s, then, the governing ethos in this country had been dramatically altered by the intellectual giants of bureaucratic theory. Because of the influence of people like Ely, Wilson, Goodnow, and Waldo, the conventional wisdom—among administrators, among academics, and even among elected officials—favored a political structure in which the traditional participants, the voters and their elected representatives, were supplemented and, indeed, superseded by the unelected and unaccountable "experts." Moreover, these experts were encouraged to apply their values in lieu of the values of the people to create a better, more efficient, and more equitable society.

The second great development for which Woodrow Wilson should be remembered is the creation of the Federal Reserve.

The late nineteenth and early twentieth centuries were characterized by a series of bank panics, the most serious one, dubbed "the Bankers' Panic" or the "Knickerbocker Crisis," taking place over a three-week span in late October and early November 1907. The severity of the crisis is debatable, as is the common-knowledge notion that J. P. Morgan personally intervened to stop the crisis, thereby demonstrating the need for a central bank. More likely, Morgan and his coterie recognized the advantages that a central bank would provide them and decided to exaggerate the severity of the 1907 crisis in order to press their advantage and advocate for one. Whatever the case, after 1907, the best and brightest in the American banking world set to work on creating an institution that would allow them to control monetary policy and provide "stability" to the economic and financial systems.

As luck would have it, they had friends in all the right places to make that happen.

The two most important players in this game were Nelson Aldrich, who was both the father-in-law of John D. Rockefeller, Jr., and the Senate majority leader; and Paul Moritz Warburg, an extremely wealthy and influential scion of the internationally powerful M. M. Warburg bank in Hamburg, Germany, and a partner at Kuhn, Loeb & Co. On the evening of November 22, 1910, these two met in Aldrich's private railway car in Hoboken, New Jersey, along with four other men: Frank A. Vanderlip, president of National City Bank of New York (now Citibank); Henry P. Davison, a senior partner in the investment bank J. P. Morgan Company; Abram Piatt Andrew, Jr., the assistant secretary of the U.S. Treasury; and Benjamin Strong, son-in-law and protégé of Edmund Converse, president of J. P. Morgan's Bankers Trust, a protégé of Davidson, and John Pierpont Morgan's personal auditor during the Panic of 1907.

The six men boarded Aldrich's railway car and left for a private resort owned by J. P. Morgan on Jekyll Island off the coast of Georgia. Under the guise of being at the resort to hunt ducks, the six locked themselves away for ten days, formulating the plan that would become the basis for the Federal Reserve System. On January 9, 1911, Aldrich introduced the plan in the Senate, claiming that it was the product of his National Monetary Commission.

The plan was met with immediate opposition, both from the Democrats and from progressive Republicans, including, most notably, President William Howard Taft, who was lukewarm on the idea, given that he did not want to seem too connected to Wall Street. The group, therefore, knew that it had two jobs, if it was going to get its proposal enacted. It would have to convince the American people, and it would have to find a president who would be more amenable to its plans.

The good news for the Jekyll Island group was that they knew they could count on Teddy Roosevelt's support. So George W. Perkins, a trusted aide to John Pierpont Morgan, encouraged his friend, the former president, to run again and to challenge Taft for the Republican nomination. The bad news was that Taft won the nomination anyway. The better news was that Perkins then encouraged Roosevelt to run under the banner of the Progressive (Bull Moose) Party, which, they knew, would cripple Taft's chances at reelection. And the best news of all was that there was a Democrat nearby whom they knew they could all support and who would, at the very least, be open to their ideas—a man who had, according to Ferdinand Lundberg, "moved in the shadow of Wall Street" for more than twenty years.[15]

That man was, of course, Woodrow Wilson, who had become quite close with several banking magnates, including the aforementioned Frank Vanderlip, one of the Jekyll Island group. Two classmates of Wilson's—Cyrus McCormick, the president of International Harvester, and Cleveland Dodge, the president of Phelps Dodge Mining—had helped him immensely in his career. They had convinced the Princeton Board of Trustees to hire Wilson, despite his intellectual radicalism. They had backed his candidacy for the presidency of the university. And they had supplemented his income since he arrived on campus from Wesleyan. More to the point, both were on the board of directors at National City Bank and were more than happy to introduce him to their friends, including Vanderlip, who would go on to become president of National City.

In 1910, Colonel George Harvey, the editor of *Harper's Weekly* and an old friend of J. P. Morgan's, helped persuade Wilson to run for governor of New Jersey, where he could ply his reformist obsession with expertise on a larger scale. Wilson agreed and, of course, won the governorship. Two years later, again at Harvey's urging, Wilson ran for president with the full support of his banker friends and others, including Jacob Schiff, another director of National City, the head of Kuhn, Loeb & Co., and the brother-in-law of Jekyll Islander Paul Warburg. Again, the pitch to Wilson was that he could ply his trade on the grandest scale of them all.

Wilson, of course, won and got right to business undermining the Constitution. Long story short, Wilson decided he wanted his "experts" to control the Federal Reserve banks (including the secretary of the treasury and the comptroller of the currency), but compromised by agreeing, essentially, to give the New York Fed to the bankers. When the Federal Reserve opened for business, Paul Warburg sat on the Board of Governors and Benjamin Strong was the governor of the New York Fed. The Aldrich plan had been changed considerably; nevertheless, two of the six members of the Jekyll Island group held prominent positions. In this way, Wilson managed to do everything a progressive positivist could want to do: He created a large, powerful central institution; he ensured that the state would maintain ultimate control over that institution; but he also ensured that the powerful private interests would be willing to supplement the government's expertise by aligning their interests with the state's. Whether he co-opted Wall Street or Wall Street co-opted him is debatable. But he won, the state won, and the bankers won. And what could be better than that?

CHAPTER 3

THE LONG MARCH THROUGH
THE INSTITUTIONS

The second part of our tale has its origins in Europe in the years after World War I. The theoretical fountainhead is located in a prison cell in Turi, Italy, in the late 1920s. The applied fountainhead is found a few years earlier, in Budapest, in the months after the end of the Great War. The two meet seamlessly, flowing through Frankfurt, Germany, in the early 1930s, and then wend their way through the institutions of the West for four-plus decades before joining the other stream, forming the *weltanschauung* in which the politicization of capital markets is not merely acceptable but necessary.

The keyword in the above paragraph is "institutions." This stream of contemporary liberalism is concerned first and foremost with institutions, loosely defined, and their effects on the broader culture. In contemporary American politics, Andrew Breitbart is, perhaps, best remembered for the astute observation that "politics is downstream from culture." And while Breitbart's aphorism was revelatory to many of his fellow conservatives, the sentiments expressed therein have been part of the accepted canon on the Left for almost a hundred years.

In 1921, the small, frail, sickly thirty-year-old editor of the socialist newspaper *L'Ordine Nuovo* (*The New Order*), a man named Antonio Gramsci, helped found the Communist Party of Italy with the backing of Soviet Premier Vladimir Lenin. A year later, Gramsci traveled to Moscow on a pilgrimage to Lenin and to work for the Comintern (aka the Third International). By the time he returned to Italy, Mussolini and his

Fascists were firmly in control of the country. In 1926, using a trumped-up attempt on his life as pretext, Mussolini enacted a handful of new security measures, including the abolition of parliamentary immunity to arrest. He had Gramsci, by then the leader of the Communist Party and a leader of the opposition in Parliament, hauled in and taken to the soon-to-be-infamous Regina Coeli prison in Rome. During his trial, the prosecutor famously remarked, "For twenty years we must stop this brain from functioning." Gramsci was first sentenced to five years, but, during the first year of that term, was given an additional twenty-year sentence and was moved to the prison at Turi.

Over the course of the next six years, before he was moved to a prison clinic at Formina, Gramsci wrote almost 3,000 pages' worth of notes, which were smuggled out to his followers. Gramsci remained a dedicated Marxist, but he wondered constantly why the revolution failed to materialize and why, moreover, everything seemed to be happening precisely backward from what one would expect, given Marx's doctrines. For starters, nationalism remained a powerful force, turning young socialists like Mussolini into fascists and enabling the entirety of Europe to fight a massive and exceptionally destructive war. Moreover, the only place where the revolution had, indeed, occurred was Russia, which, according to Marx, should have been the last place to revolt, given its lack of industrialization. Clearly, something was wrong with the Communist theology, but what?

What Gramsci concluded, more or less, is that it's awfully tough to start a new religion where an existing religion is already firmly entrenched. He didn't put it that way, of course. He said that Marx was wrong in his presumption that all of man's history is the story of economic class conflict. Rather, Gramsci argued that the real class conflicts are cultural, which, in turn, led to a theory of cultural revolution. The battle for the soul of mankind must be waged on cultural grounds first, and only after the existing culture has been thoroughly destroyed can the new culture—and the new economics—be established.[1]

Like Marx, Gramsci saw Christianity as an enemy, although for Gramsci the religion's influence was much more pervasive and much more corrosive. Christianity, you see, was not just a faith, but a cultural force, the creator and enabler of the bourgeois culture that kept the classes living relatively peacefully and harmoniously with one another.

Therefore, in order to bring about the revolution and liberate the workers of the world from their chains, both the Christian Church and the Christian culture had to be destroyed. As the enigmatic and controversial priest-turned-writer Malachi Martin put it in his analysis of Gramsci and his ideas: "There would be no Marxist-inspired violent overthrow of the ruling 'superstructure' by the working 'underclasses.' Because no matter how oppressed they might be, the 'structure' of the working classes was defined not by their misery or their oppression but by their Christian faith and their Christian culture."[2]

In light of all of this, Gramsci believed that the proletarian revolution must be preceded by a cultural revolution, one in which the anti-Christian Marxists made what the German Marxist student leader Rudi Dutschke would later call "the long march through the institutions."

While Gramsci was still editing Communist newspapers, in Budapest a young Communist agitator named Bela Kun was taking control of Hungary, which was fresh from a loss in the Great War and the dissolution of its alliance with Austria. Kun fought for the Austro-Hungarian Empire during the war, was captured by Russian forces, and was sent to a POW camp somewhere in the Urals. When the Revolution broke out, Kun was freed and decided to stay on and fight with the Bolsheviks, earning a reputation as someone even Lenin thought was a radical. Kun returned to Hungary and, in time, established the Hungarian Soviet Republic.

While the Hungarian Soviet Republic proved to be short-lived, it nevertheless produced one towering figure, György Lukács, an intellectual and erstwhile Romantic literary critic whose conversion to Communism came just in time to join Kun's Communist Party and to serve as the deputy people's commissar for education and culture in the new Hungarian Soviet Republic. In his biography of Lukács, Victor Zitta described the efforts the education and culture commissar undertook during his reign to ensure the "proper" education of the next generation of Hungarian Communists as follows:

> Special lectures were organized in schools and literature printed and distributed to "instruct" children about free love, about the nature of sexual intercourse, about the archaic nature of bourgeois family codes, about the outdatedness of monogamy, and the irrelevance of religion,

which deprives man of all pleasure. Children urged thus to reject and deride paternal authority and the authority of the Church, and to ignore precepts of morality, easily and spontaneously turned into delinquents with whom only the police could cope....This call to rebellion addressed to children was matched by a call to rebellion addressed to Hungarian women.[3]

When the Hungarian experiment in Soviet Communism ended 133 days later, Lukács stayed behind, clandestinely, to help reorganize the party, but eventually fled to Vienna, where he would stay, in exile, for the next decade.

In 1923, Lukács published his foundational Communist work, *History and Class Consciousness*. Because of this book, Lukács is generally considered the founding father of "Western" or "cultural" Marxism. His interpretation of Marx's notions of reification (a special case of alienation) and commodity fetishism (a special case of reification) developed, in much greater detail, the idea that man's consciousness is dissociated at a fundamental level from society. In turn, that means that society itself is an alienating entity, and if man is to overcome the reification of his consciousness, society itself must first be altered. In practical terms, then, Lukács's best known and most influential work both endorses the Gramscian explanation for the Communist revolution's failure to occur and sets the stage for subsequent stronger and more fundamental critiques of Western society.

All things considered, Lukács's greatest contribution to the ongoing Marxist dialog was quite probably his introduction of an aesthetics component to Marxian thought, thereby altering the very nature of the Socialist worldview. By adding this aesthetic component to Socialism/ Communism, Lukács turned Marxism into a philosophical endeavor, replete with explicit normative value judgments, abandoning Engels and the purported scientific impartiality of Socialist economics to the Russian Soviets.

Lukács quickly became the most prominent and most important thinker in the Hungarian underground in Vienna. While there, he met and shared ideas with many of the young Marxists of the era, including, notably, Antonio Gramsci.

The same year that *History and Class Consciousness* was published, a man named Felix Weil received his doctorate from Goethe University Frankfurt, writing his dissertation on the practical problems of implementing Socialism. Weil was from a wealthy Argentinian family, and not long after graduating, he financed a weeklong symposium in Frankfurt that was attended by Lukács and some twenty-plus other like-minded intellectuals, with "the hope that the different trends in Marxism, if afforded an opportunity of talking it out together, could arrive at a 'true' or 'pure' Marxism." The meeting was organized by Weil's professor Karl Korsch, a prominent German Marxist. The event was so successful that Weil decided to support an ongoing discussion of these subjects. He funded what we today would call a "think tank," dedicated exclusively to the study of Marxism as a scientific discipline. Its formal name was the Institute for Social Research, although it would come to be known, simply, as the Frankfurt School.

The Frankfurt School, in turn, became the "iskra" for Cultural Marxism. Iskra is the Russian word for "spark" and the term that Lenin used for the bloc of bourgeois intellectuals (like himself) whose intervention was necessary to awaken the masses and thus to "spark" the revolution. Under the leadership of Max Horkheimer, a Marxist professor of philosophy, the focus of the School shifted from uncovering the problems of Marxism to an activist-oriented and typically utopian agenda of liberating "human beings from the circumstances that enslave them." Horkheimer called this process "critical theory," which he said was different from traditional Marxist theories because its purpose was to critique and change society rather than simply try to explain or understand it. He put it this way: "[Critical Theory] is not just a research hypothesis which shows its value in the ongoing business of men; it is an essential element in the historical effort to create a world which satisfies the needs and powers of men."[4]

The German professor Jürgen Habermas, a second-generation Frankfurt School philosopher, explained critical theory this way: "[Horkheimer developed it] to think through political disappointments at the absence of revolution in the West, the development of Stalinism in Soviet Russia, and the victory of fascism in Germany. It was supposed to explain mistaken Marxist prognoses, but without breaking Marxist intentions."[5]

In 1933, when Hitler became chancellor of Germany, Horkheimer moved the Institute to Geneva, then to Paris, and finally, in 1935, to New York City, where it affiliated with Columbia University.

The Lukács-Frankfurt School's social reinterpretation of Marxism is important, not just in an academic sense, but in a much broader, much more practical sense as well, which is precisely how they wanted it. Horkheimer's interpretation of the state of Marxism was more pessimistic than even Lukács's or Gramsci's. He saw the situation in Europe in the direst of terms. There would never be any revolution if he and his colleagues did not first figure out how to undo the cultural and psychological bourgeois hegemony.

Following Lukács's lead, the Frankfurt School was explicitly anti-positivist, which is to say that it rejected Hume's Newtonian approach to social phenomena, Marx's "scientific socialism," Comte's positivism, and the American Progressives' scientism. Instead, the Frankfurt "critical theorists" harkened back directly to Rousseau and to his belief that man, in the state of nature, is perfect. Perhaps the most famous line Rousseau ever wrote was the first line in the first chapter of *The Social Contract*: "Man is born free; and everywhere he is in chains." This, then, is the rub. Man is free in nature but is chained by society, which is an artificial construct that suppresses his true nature, oppresses him, and keeps him from achieving that to which he is entitled.

To explain why the European workers did not revolt, why the very idea of revolutions seemed to them to be unwise, Horkheimer and his colleague Theodor Adorno took Lukács's antipositivism one step further, digging down deep into the idea of men—workers, the bourgeoisie, the moneyed class, whoever—as actors in and *on* society, not just the passive victims of Marx's historical trends. To do so, they incorporated the works and theories of psychoanalysis into their interpretations of history, economics, and mankind. Specifically, they looked to Freud.

In his classic tome *Modern Times*, the great British historian Paul Johnson argues that the three horsemen of the modern apocalypse all affected the modern world deeply and profoundly. "Marx, Freud, and Einstein," Johnson wrote, "all conveyed the same message to the 1920s: the world was not what it seemed. The senses, whose empirical perceptions shaped our ideas of time and distance, right and wrong, law and justice, and the nature of man's behavior in society were not to be trusted."[6]

It is no surprise, therefore, that the critical theorists of the Frankfurt School turned to Freud. Freud and psychoanalysis could help explain how and why the workers of the world refused to unite. And as luck would have it, Freud had already done much of their work for them, creating a worldview that explained man's cultural and psychological dissociation from his real nature and his true interests. Freud's *Civilization and Its Discontents* argued that civilization is a false reality, an artificially constructed edifice designed to suppress the id. To the critical theorists, capitalism was the creator of this false reality, this false consciousness, which robbed man of his creativity and spontaneity, providing him a veneer of "comfort" in their stead. Therefore, if man was ever to be truly happy, ever able to be what nature intended him to be, he would first have to shed the false consciousness of capitalism's self-interested civilization.

Or to put it another way, the Frankfurt School and its critical theorists integrated Freud's social psychology with Rousseau's state of nature fetishization, Gramsci's aggressive anti-Christianity, and Lukács's detestation of social and sexual mores to fashion the "Cultural Marxism" that would become the dominant ideology of the New Left in America and, by extension, of the entire American system of higher education.

When the Frankfurt School arrived in the United States, setting down roots at Columbia University in 1935, it landed on fertile ground. Between the Fabians and the Bloomsburies in Great Britain, Marxism had become the accepted worldview of the avant-garde in the arts, the humanities, and even economics. The philosopher G. E. Moore's 1903 book *Principia Ethica* formed the foundation of a new "secular religion" that defined "liberty" in purely libertine terms and defined ethics in purely emotive terms. The net effect of the two was an educated elite who saw existing Judeo-Christian morality as part of the false consciousness of civilization and believed that a new and better morality should be defined exclusively by their feelings. John Maynard Keynes, the economic architect of Roosevelt's New Deal and a member of the Bloomsbury Group, freely admitted that "one of the greatest advantages of [Moore's] religion, was that it made morals unnecessary...."[7]

The Fabians, and especially the Bloomsburies, had significant reach and deeply affected the fields in which they practiced, from art to literature to economics, on both sides of the Atlantic. Keynes's *General Theory of Employment, Interest and Money* was published the year after the Frankfurt School arrived at Columbia, but the seeds of the academy's leftward tilt were sown long before. The long march through the institutions had begun, in other words, but it was incomplete.

When the critical theorists first arrived in the United States, they continued to publish in German, which they rightly deemed important, because they were the only organization that freely published intellectual texts and inquiries in German during the Nazis' reign. This limited their impact in the United States, however, leaving their operation, dedicated to the long march, isolated politically and academically. Max Horkheimer and Theodor Adorno continued to produce important and intellectually challenging work, most notably their *Dialectic of Enlightenment*, which contained a savage critique of positivism and reinforced their status as the leaders of the psychoanalytical subgenre of Marxist thought. But they had little impact outside of intellectual circles.

In 1949, Horkheimer, still the leader of the Frankfurt School, packed up shop and took the Institute back to Frankfurt. He was followed in short order by Adorno, who was, by that time, interested primarily in aesthetics and music. And that, more or less, would have been the end of the Frankfurt School's American influence, were it not for one thing, one unfortunate coincidence that changed the American academic and political scene entirely.

In 1951, a German-American mathematician named Sophie Wertheim passed away from cancer. She left behind her grown son, who was studying law at Yale, and her husband of twenty-seven years, who had, for the last decade, worked for the U.S. government, first as part of William Donovan's "brain trust" at the Office of Strategic Services (the precursor to the CIA) and then at the State Department. When his wife passed, the man, who held a PhD from the University of Freiberg, left government service and went back to his first love, academics. After short stints at Columbia and Harvard, he settled down in Waltham, Massachusetts, where he taught at Brandeis for seven years before escaping to sunny Southern California, where he would finish out his career at the University of San Diego.

This man—Herbert Marcuse—would drastically change American education and culture, leaving behind a world much different and much more politically preoccupied than it had been and, for that matter, much more than it should be.

At Freiberg, Marcuse had known and studied under Martin Heidegger, who was soon to become the most important philosopher in the *other* half of the Leftist Continental school of philosophy and the principal proto-postmodernist. Marcuse's academic career floundered, however, as the Nazis rose to power, and he wound up finding a home at the Frankfurt School, just in time to go into exile. He taught and wrote as part of the Frankfurt School for seven years before joining the U.S. government to aid the war effort. He consciously and purposely stayed behind in the United States when the Institute, along with Horkheimer and Adorno, moved back to Germany. At the time, Herbert Marcuse was largely unknown outside a small circle of academics. But all of that was about to change.

In 1959, Marcuse published his first major work in years, *Eros and Civilization*, which was derived from a series of lectures he had given and had dedicated to his late wife. In it, Marcuse fully fused Gramscian false consciousness and Marxian critical theory with Freudian notions of sexual repression and sublimation to conclude, in essence, that the key to undermining bourgeois society and thereby ending man's false understanding of his reality is sexual liberation and perversion. The theory was unremarkable, historically speaking, merely repeating the trite heresies of the Brethren of the Free Spirit and countless other medieval millenarian movements[8] and the Bloomsburies, among others. Nevertheless, the book would, in time, become one of the rationalizing texts of the sexual revolution. As the conservative intellectual (and publisher of this book) Roger Kimball put it:

> [I]n *Eros and Civilization* (1959)—a book that became a bible of the counterculture—Marcuse spins a fairy tale about the fate of man in industrial society. Like Brown, he conjures up the image of a "non-repressive reality principle" in which "the body in its entirety would become...an instrument of pleasure." What this really amounts to is a form of infantilization. Marcuse speaks glowingly of "a resurgence of pregenital polymorphous sexuality" that "protests against the repressive order of procreative sexuality." He recommends returning to a state of "primary narcissism" in which one will find "the redemption of

pleasure, the halt of time, the absorption of death; silence, sleep, night, paradise—the Nirvana principle not as death but as life." In other words, he looks forward to a community of solipsists.

Marcuse is explicit about the social implications of his experiment in narcissism. "This change in the value and scope of libidinal relations," he writes, "would lead to a disintegration of the institutions in which the private interpersonal relations have been organized, particularly the monogamic and patriarchal family." That is to say, ultimate liberation is indistinguishable from ultimate self-absorption.[9]

In 1964, Marcus published his seminal work, *The One-Dimensional Man*, in which he argued that modern technocratic society was crushing man's spirit and making him one-dimensional. Modern capitalism was crushing man's capacity for critical thought and oppositional behavior. The following year, he published the article "Repressive Tolerance," in which he argued that certain forms of speech—reactionary, conservative—should be repressed in the name of *genuine* tolerance.

The conventional wisdom holds that Marcuse—with his advocacy of free love, sexual perversion, oppositional behavior, and suppression of "reactionary" thought—was the intellectual father of the New Left. But this wasn't exactly the case. Marcuse, like nearly all German philosophers and everyone else associated with the Frankfurt School, wrote extremely dense and turgid prose. The concepts he discussed were complicated and difficult to follow. Paul Breines, a student activist from the University of Wisconsin (and, in time, a professor at Boston College), noted the misunderstanding surrounding Marcuse's role in the New Left in his 1968 contribution to a book on the philosopher, edited by Jurgen Habermas. "One-Dimensional Man and the Repressive Tolerance essay," Breines wrote, "remain unread by large portions of the Left; only a very small percentage has, or cares to have, more than the vaguest comprehension of the philosophical tradition in which Marcuse stands."

Marcuse was, more than anything, a media creation. When the Students for a Democratic Society (SDS) and other student radicals began disrupting campuses and rioting in 1968, Marcuse was one of the few academics who openly and assertively supported their actions. Because his ideas, in many ways, presaged the radicals' ideas, most of the students—and all of the media—were familiar with Marcuse only superficially. He became the "guru" and the "founder" of the movement, even though most of its participants—including its leader, Tom Hayden—knew almost nothing about him or critical theory.

The thing that Marcuse provided the New Left was intellectual legitimacy. Rather than a bunch of bored kids running around, screwing everything in sight, experimenting with drugs, and trying desperately to avoid serving their country in war, Marcuse made the movement "respectable." Why, the media would gush, the New Left is not just a bunch of self-absorbed, spoiled children trying to tear down the structures of society in pursuit of their own libidinal and hedonistic pleasure. They're serious and intelligent people, with serious and intelligent ideas, and serious and intelligent complaints, led by the most serious and most intelligent man around. Dismiss them if you want, but you'd be much better off to "stop, hey, what's that sound; everybody look what's goin' down."

Marcuse's newfound fame and the ongoing radicalism of the various student movements prompted two men, in particular, to dig deeper into the thoughts behind the "guru" of the New Left. The first of these was a philosopher at the University of New York at Buffalo named Paul Piccone. Piccone started a journal called *Telos*, in which he dug into Marcuse's older works and those of the other theorists of the Frankfurt School, resurrecting their ideas and bringing them to a new audience.

The second was a PhD student in history at Harvard named Martin Jay, who wrote his dissertation on the Frankfurt School. The dissertation was published as a book called *The Dialectical Imagination*. Jay's book was an immediate hit—at least among a certain crowd. Like Piccone, Jay capitalized on Marcuse's fame to resurrect the Frankfurt thinkers for a new generation, most of whom knew Marcuse only as a "radical" intellectual.

In the preface to the 1996 edition of his book, Jay wrote that it "was written…in the hope of facilitating [the reception and embrace of Critical Theory and the Frankfurt School], but without inviting the uncritical dogmatism that characterized so many other embraces of Marxist theory." He concluded that, in that sense, he had succeeded far beyond his most "grandiose fantasies."[10]

Jay's book was, more or less, the *Reader's Digest* version of Critical Theory, which is to say that he took the complex ideas and theories of the Frankfurt School and turned them into easily digestible bits. These bits were then immediately scarfed down by a hungry pseudo-intellectual audience that was desperately searching for intellectual gravitas to support the radicalism of the 1960s and 1970s.

Suddenly, Critical Theory was all the rage, and American universities couldn't get enough of this newly rediscovered line of Marxist thought. As Thomas Wheatland, a history professor at Assumption College, noted in his 2009 book *The Frankfurt School in Exile*, "Although they wrote and lectured about an Intellect tradition critical of most aspects of U.S. society, scholars of the Frankfurt School were invited into the establishment, earning chairs at such prestigious universities as Harvard, Yale, Princeton, Cornell, Columbia, Duke, the University of California at Berkeley, and the University of Chicago."[11]

Everybody, everywhere in American academia wanted to be a radical and a Critical Theorist. As Critical Theory became a core part of the curriculum, so other aspects of the New Left became institutionalized as well. Suddenly, postmodernism was a respectable field rather than the mad rantings of disappointed Stalinists. Identity politics took hold as well, as the feminists, the sexual theorists, and race theorists all demanded their own intellectual outlets. As the aforementioned Paul Piccone noted sadly in 1988, "Western Marxism, Critical Theory, and radical philosophy in general have smoothly blended into the otherwise bland, jargon-ridden and hopelessly conventional framework they originally challenged."[12]

Piccone, obviously, was unhappy about this development. He considered Critical Theory and the Frankfurt School to be something new, unique, and exceptionally powerful. He had hoped for more from it than simply seeing it become a dumbed-down version of every other Marxian intellectual endeavor. And while one can certainly sympathize with his disappointment, it is actually the case that he had the whole thing backward.

The Frankfurt School didn't fail. It succeeded remarkably. Thanks to the media savvy of Marcuse, the brilliant intellectual storytelling of Martin Jay, the mistaken idealism of the 1960s student radicals, and the intellectual vacuousness of the American educational establishment, Marxist Critical Theory, along with all of the other half-baked Marxian-derived intellectual enterprises, became one of the foundational ideologies of the American university.

By conquering the American university the Critical Theorists, and especially Marcuse, managed to do precisely what Gramsci and Lukács had suggested needed doing a half-century earlier. They stripped away the veneer of false consciousness—or, more accurately, they stripped away the consciousness that had existed previously, replacing it with their own consciousness, one rooted in skepticism and alienation, which would become the overarching themes in higher education and every single endeavor subsequently undertaken by those who passed through the American system of higher education from the 1970s on. Thomas Wheaton, in the conclusion of his *Frankfurt School in Exile,* argues that "'The long march through the institutions' which Rudi Dutschke and Herbert Marcuse envisioned, was accomplished, but, surprisingly, it was by invitation."[13]

Wheaton is correct, though one might be forgiven for questioning his surprise. This was the plan all along. And while it happened in an unusual and unexpected manner—blending the mass-marketing of a new-age sage with an arcane academic methodology and a traditional Marxist student movement—it happened nonetheless.

Moreover, the fact that it didn't translate immediately into the new, more authentic consciousness of the theoretical myth wasn't taken as disproof of the myth, but of the need to "do more," which is precisely what the unwittingly and unknowingly indoctrinated are busy doing.

CHAPTER 4

WHERE TWO STREAMS MEET

By the late 1960s and the early 1970s, it seemed that the world had been changed, forever and irreversibly. What one thought about those changes—whether they were good or bad—largely depended on such variables as socioeconomic status, education level, partisan political predisposition, and, of course, age. In general, the younger, the wealthier, the better educated, and the more Democratic-leaning one was, the more likely he or she would be to see the changes of the era in a positive light.

The far Left—Socialists, Communists, and other fellow travelers—had, as we have seen, successfully navigated their long march through the institutions. The two trends in American society identified in the previous two chapters—the positivist co-optation of religious rhetoric and managerial practice and the inculcation of the American education establishment with the idea that traditional American culture is a bourgeois false reality—completely changed the nation and nearly all of its institutions.

After Wilson's Social Gospel presidency, mainline Protestantism and much of American Catholicism integrated their visions for God's children on Earth with the political Left's vision of government as the principal force for good in American society. As Reinhold Niebuhr drifted slowly away from the hardcore socialism of his youth to the more mainstream, anti-Communist statism of the post-war Democrats, much of American Christianity followed. By the end of the 1960s, much of mainline Christianity had been either subsumed by the proactive state or had fallen from faith altogether. Likewise, the Catholic Church had been transformed by Vatican II, and even the Southern Baptist Convention was drifting slowly to the Left.

In brief, the social, political, educational, and political trends that had dominated the previous century reached a critical mass in the years that more or less coincided with the Vietnam War. These trends blended with one another to create a new American *weltanschauung* that would come to dominate the social and political scenes. This worldview was based on a host of often contradictory principles, all adopted perfunctorily and pointedly, with the goal being the attainment and consolidation of power. They included the fetishization of scientific principles; the belief that American traditionalism was inhibiting and selfish; faith in the power of external entities, like the state or other large organizations, to change the status quo for the better; and a tacit rejection of self-government, which is to say a belief that "the people" are, in most cases, either ignorant of the expertise required to function effectively or too selfish and self-serving to face their false consciousness, and thus require leadership on the part of an enlightened elite.

As these two "streams" of American political and social thought merged in the late 1970s, they fed off one another and became a raging torrent, washing over virtually the entirety of American society. The battle for the hearts and minds of America seemed won. Americans were ready to throw off their false consciousness and emerge into the glory of their new, fairer, and more just existence. Only one thing now stood in the way of the emergence of the "New American Man," namely the Old American Man. The Old American Man was, for the most part, pretty happy. Sure, there were problems, but then, Utopia doesn't exist, which the Old American Man knew, but the New American man refused to believe.

Far and away the thing that kept the Old American Man grounded was business. He had a job, likely a good job. He got up in the morning, went to work, came home, had dinner with his family, went to bed, and got up to repeat the whole cycle afresh, five days a week. And it was all made possible by American business. As Calvin Coolidge famously put it, "The chief business of the American people is business. They are profoundly concerned with producing, buying, selling, investing, and prospering in the world." America and business were inextricably linked.

But that, too, was about to change. The two streams that had become a torrent would soon wash over everything and, as they did, would leave their silt and mold on everything they touched. Business was strong, and business could resist the decomposition that the constant battering would precipitate—but it could not do so forever.

The same process that overtook the rest of American society also played out in American business. The process here began in much the same way and at much the same time as it did with the other institutions. In the early twentieth century Frederick Winslow Taylor, a wealthy industrialist, sought to fix the problems of the world by adapting "scientific" theories to the field of business. Taylor's "scientific" ideas weren't exactly "scientific" as we understand the term, but they were rational and empirical, and, as such, many of them were solid and beneficial in the context of manufacturing and business operations. But when it came to the human aspects of business administration, Taylor's ideas were as useless as Wilson's were to the human aspects of government administration.

The key difference between Taylor's ideas and those of his contemporaries (and the reason why he was not included in the history of "scientific" administration) is that his thoughts on business practices could be easily separated from his beliefs about epistemology and methodology, meaning that many of his ideas maintained their empirical merit, in addition to or *in spite of* his normative predispositions. Efficiency, standardization, best practices, and knowledge-transfer between workers were all principles that could be incorporated into business management, generally enhancing business productivity and success. These techniques couldn't (and didn't) yield a single "best way" to manage businesses, as Taylor had theorized they would, but they did improve business performance. As a result, there was—and is—considerable value in Taylor's codification of business management practices. Conscious, empirical, and methodical assessment of strengths, weaknesses, opportunities, and threats is both sensible and effective.

In the boom years after World War II, companies and their leaders began to think about ways to improve their long-term success. By the late 1940s and early 1950s, corporate planning managers had become *de rigueur* in American business. In 1962, a man named Robert Stewart, who had worked in corporate planning for Lockheed, put together a team of researchers at the Stanford Research Institute (SRI) in Menlo Park, California.

Over the course of the decade during which he ran the program— called the "Theory and Practice of Planning" program (or TAPP, for short)—Stewart hired engineers, businessmen, planners, and various others, all of whom he thought could bring different perspectives to the project, the principal goal of which was to answer the "planning paradox." The paradox, put simply, posits that planning is necessary and important but is hardly sufficient for business success; rigid adherence to prior plans can cause businesses to miss opportunities and engage in poor decision-making.[1]

In 1963, TAPP issued its first report, "A Framework For Business Planning," which not only became the foundational blueprint for the work that the group would conduct over the next decade, but also introduced some of the most important concepts in business management since Taylor's work a half-century earlier. Among the concepts developed by TAPP and introduced remedially in this report was a decision-matrix and an analytical method named for and using the variables mentioned above—strengths, weaknesses, opportunities, and threats—which came to be known by the acronym "SWOT."[2]

While SWOT is a methodological idea developed in the broader epistemological framework of strategic planning, a second concept, a sub-category of strategic planning, in which the SWOT technique would be applied by Stewart and TAPP, was something they called "stakeholder" planning, a term coined by team member Marion Doscher. The idea was to chart the course of the company, to plan strategically by analyz- ing input on strengths, weaknesses, opportunities, and threats from a variety of "stakeholder" groups, each of which would have a different interest in the company—shareholders, customers, employees, manag- ers, unions, and so on. A logical and natural extension of the idea of strategic planning, stakeholder analysis was intended to force managers and executives to see how their decisions affected different groups and how best to handle an array of often conflicting and competing interests. The idea—which seems entirely commonsensical in retrospect—was that it would be difficult, if not impossible, to plan effectively for the future without knowing what customers, employees, and others might need and want in the future.

This is an important point to remember: When stakeholder analysis was introduced, it was introduced as an analytical tool, the means by which the managers of organizations could better understand their organization's position in its environment and, thus, better understand how to solidify and improve that position. Additionally, it's important to remember that the Stanford Research Institute was not, and is not, an academic institution. Rather, it is a practical research organization. It is affiliated with an academic institution, obviously, but it nevertheless had and has clients in the business world who are looking for practical advice and help, not theoretical concepts.

Given this, once Stewart et al. had developed their analytical framework, they began presenting it to clients, some individually, others in seminars. By 1970, TAPP had trained at least 600 students from at least 300 organizations in its Business Executive Seminars.[3]

In 1967, one of the TAPP team members, a Harvard Business School graduate and former Boeing manager named Albert Humphrey, contacted Professor Kenneth R. Andrews at Harvard to discuss TAPP's materials and to ask if the Business School would be interested in learning more. Andrews replied to Humphrey that he found the material interesting, that Harvard was aware of the TAPP team's work, and that the school's business policy course already utilized some of their methodologies, as did the textbook written for the course, the hugely influential *Business Policy: Text and Cases*. The cooperation between SRI and Harvard Business School was important, not just because it meant that the tools developed at SRI were being successfully mainstreamed, but also because it pulled the ideas out of the purely practical realm and deposited them in the academic realm as well. Harvard Business School was the training ground for the best and the brightest in American business. And while it focused on practical, concrete "training" more than pure academics, it was nonetheless much more a part of the academic milieu than was SRI.[4]

In 1971, Stewart retired. The next year, Humphrey started his own business management consultancy and helped expand the reach of the SRI tactical and strategic concepts far beyond the walls of SRI. Within a few years, these concepts were everywhere. Indeed, in a 1974 article titled "American Finance: Three Views of Strategy" and published in the *Journal of General Management*, Israel Unterman confirmed that TAPP's methods were being used throughout American industry, including American finance companies like Chase Manhattan.[5,6]

During the 1970s, as the business planning and strategic management fields matured, the term "stakeholder" faded somewhat from the literature. Nevertheless, the concept was internalized by corporate executives, directors, planners, and educators. McKinsey & Company developed a four-stage maturity model to describe and assess the sophistication of corporate planning and strategy processes, with the most "mature" stages including consideration of "external" forces and actors. The "Harvard Policy Model" became more clearly defined—and notably included SWOT analysis.

In a groundbreaking article in the February 1975 edition of *Long Range Planning*, William R. Dill, then the dean of New York University's Graduate School of Business Administration, made the case, now obvious in retrospect, that the relationship between corporations and stakeholders is not a one-way street, that corporate decisions and actions affect stakeholders who then respond by changing their perceptions and demands of the corporation. "For a long time, we have assumed that the views and initiatives of stakeholders could be dealt with as externalities to the strategic planning," Dill wrote. "We have been reluctant, though, to admit the idea that some of these outside stakeholders might seek and earn active roles with management to make decisions." That was a mistake, Dill suggested, one that was rightfully being corrected. Thus, he concluded, "The move of today is from stakeholder influence toward stakeholder participation."[7]

In 1979, Mariann Jelinek published her important and illustrative study of strategic planning, *Institutionalizing Innovation: A Study of Organizational Learning Systems*. In it, she argued that strategic planning was a continuation of the work started by Frederick Winslow Taylor, the "systemization" of corporate behavior, only applied to the C-Suite rather than the factory floor. In so doing, she made the case that strategic planning, including all actors and assessing all needs, could formalize the processes of corporate management, accounting for and accommodating all externalities. "It is through administrative systems that planning and policy are made possible because the systems capture knowledge about the task," Jelinek wrote. And so, "true management by exception, and true policy direction are now possible, solely because management is no longer wholly immersed in the details of the task itself."[8]

By the end of the decade, then, strategic planning literature and practice had evolved along familiar lines. Initial success in utilizing scientific principles of observation and harnessing those to the power of mathematic modeling had yielded significant improvement over past practices and seemed to create a complete and systematically effective means for addressing the pitfalls of corporate strategic planning. Most notably, this systemic approach both understood the importance of external actors—i.e., stakeholders—and incorporated their involvement in and impact on the function of a business.

By the end of the 1970s, the stakeholder subgenre of strategic planning and business management—although yet still largely unnamed—had evolved through *two* distinct iterations. It began as a purely "descriptive" or "empirical" exercise, whereby observers—usually corporate managers—identified the key players and the key drivers involved in a specific corporation's behavior, for example, executives, managers, the corporation itself, customers, employees, and board members.

The second iteration, which grew naturally out of the first, was called the "instrumental" model, and is defined as the process by which the data or empirical observations gathered by the descriptive model are utilized to assess the impact of stakeholder connections and to determine whether the existing pattern of relationships is contributing to or detracting from traditional goals. For example, does a business's employment policy encourage employees to work harder and more efficiently for their managers? Does its executive pay structure incentivize or disincentivize employee morale? Do its environmental practices attract or repel customers? And so on.[9]

In a 1995 article describing the evolution of the stakeholder model, Thomas Donaldson and Lee Preston noted that "Whatever their methodologies, these studies have tended to generate 'implications' suggesting that adherence to stakeholder principles and practices achieves conventional corporate performance objectives as well or better than rival approaches."[10] What this tells us, then, is that stakeholder theory had become a key concept in corporate strategic analysis and planning. This confirms not only that the idea was always intended to be a descriptive and analytical tool, but also that it was a tool that successful companies had already begun using to give themselves an advantage. Donaldson and Preston continued, "[H]ighly successful companies as Hewlett Packard, Wal-Mart, and Dayton Hudson—although very diverse in other ways—share a stakeholder perspective. Kotter and Heskett wrote that '[a]lmost all [their] managers care strongly about people who have a stake in the business—customers, employees, stockholders, suppliers, etc.'"[11]

Of course, the catch with the descriptive and instrumental models of stakeholder theory is that they applied purely systemic, scientific methodologies to phenomena that were not easily shoehorned into a scientific framework. In a well-known article for the *Harvard Business Review*, management Professor Henry Mintzberg suggested that strategic planning in general suffered from three key fallacies: *the fallacy of prediction*, which, of course, rightly acknowledges that business managers are no different from anyone else and are thus unable to look into the future and see what it will bring; *the fallacy of detachment*, which describes the inherent difficulty in enabling plan-makers and plan-implementers to see events and processes from the same perspective, each with perfect knowledge of the other; and *the fallacy of formalization*, which is the fallacy common to all positivist endeavors, the presumption that the "system" can process corporate actions and goals better and more effectively than can a human, who is able to assess new information as it becomes available and adjust accordingly.[12]

All of this should be rather familiar by now. As with public management and the social sciences more generally, there is an obvious flaw in the business management/strategic planning epistemology, one drawn largely from the fact that human activity, interactions, and decision-making processes tend to defy systemization. The little human animal has a mind of his own and defies behaving in ways that fit the statistical model.

As a result, by the start of the 1980s, many in the field of strategic planning had come to the conclusion that they had to figure out how to develop their methodology in ways that accounted for human interactions. Again, like the public administrators and the social scientists before them, the business strategists had to acknowledge that every decision is, by definition, derived from a normative judgment of some sort, an expression of preference and value.

As all this was taking place in Menlo Park, Cambridge, Wall Street, London, and countless other locations around the world, a young man named R. Edward Freeman had just completed his PhD in philosophy at Washington University in St. Louis and took a job as a researcher at the Wharton Business School at the University of Pennsylvania. Within a few months, Freeman was part of a new splinter group at Wharton called the Wharton Applied Research Center, which was set up to operate like a real-world consulting company in the image of, although without the heavy hitters at, SRI.[13] Through his work, Freeman became familiar with the problems faced by business managers and executives, as well as the real-world shortcomings of the existing largely positivistic approach to strategic management. He also became familiar with the concept of "stakeholder" modeling and with the idea that corporate managers and executives needed ways to determine whom and what their businesses affected and how best to utilize that knowledge to run those businesses more effectively. As Freeman put it, he had three primary questions at the time: "(i) Could one develop a method for executives to strategically manage stakeholder relationships as a routine ongoing part of their day-to-day activities? (ii) Could strategic management as a discipline be recast along stakeholder lines rather than as the six tasks of Schendel and Hofer? And (iii) Why was any of this thinking controversial, since it seemed to be complete 'common sense'...?"[14]

Not coincidentally, while conducting strategy seminars and learning about how companies, executives, and managers dealt with various stakeholder groups, Freeman became friendly with a man named William Evan, a sociologist at UPenn. Evan saw Freeman's work not just in empirical terms, but in normative terms as well, which is to say that he saw the stakeholder model as "a way to democratize the large corporation."[15] Evan and Freeman planned a book together, addressing the "ethics of capitalism."[16] And while the book was never completed, the collaboration produced a handful of articles. More to the point, it not only addressed the inherent weaknesses in the positivist, scientific aspects of the strategic planning model, but it also opened Freeman's eyes to the possibilities hiding in his erstwhile tactical model.

In 1984, Freeman published the founding document in normative strategic planning, *Strategic Management: A Stakeholder Approach.* Freeman's recourse to normative appeals was relatively mild, but it did set a precedent as well as acknowledge a shortcoming. As he made the case that ethical and social issues are all part of a strategic plan to please stakeholders and manage a company most effectively, Freeman acknowledged the shortcomings of the existing model and also encouraged those who would study his methods to incorporate their own normative concerns into their work. Freeman revived the field of strategic planning by enlarging its mission and making it less overtly objective and more abstract and theoretical. He killed the patient to save it—as someone had to and as someone eventually would, in any case.

Now, if you think you've heard this story before, that's because you have. To reiterate: This is precisely the progression noted earlier with respect to both public management and the social sciences. What began as a useful heuristic was determined to be insufficient in addressing broader sociological questions because it utilized a methodology incompatible with the vicissitudes of human interaction. Once this is determined to be the case—and it is always the case—the observer has two options for dealing with the revelation. He may either scale back the ambition of his observational interests and agree that he will observe only that which he is empirically capable of observing; or he may push onward, agreeing that the methodology is flawed and agreeing, therefore, to correct it by allowing for the introduction of non-objective, value-laden variables. From there, the questions to be answered become exclusively value-directed, changing the conversation from one about how best to codify and utilize observations to one about which values to incorporate into the model to produce the best observations.

The aforementioned Donaldson and Preston noted that this third iteration of stakeholder analysis, the "normative" model, created an entirely new set of advantages but also an entirely new set of problems.

Among the most important problems with the development of the normative model was the fact that many in the field of strategic planning and stakeholder analysis failed to disclose the differences between this model and the others, which is to say that they failed to explain the differences between what *is* or what *could* be and what *should* be. "A striking characteristic of the stakeholder literature is that diverse theoretical approaches are often combined without acknowledgment."[17] This led, in turn, to poor analysis at both the academic and business levels, making a mess of the whole idea of stakeholder analysis. "The muddling of theoretical bases and objectives, although often understandable, has led to less rigorous thinking and analysis than the stakeholder concept requires."[18] Finally, all of this created an environment in which stakeholder analysis was discussed and undertaken with rote repetition of "values," many of which were inapplicable or contraindicated by circumstances. "Much of the stakeholder literature, including the contributions of both proponents and critics, is clearly normative, although the fundamental normative principles involved are often unexamined."[19]

By moving the business strategy debate beyond what is observable, the stakeholder theorists may have addressed their own need for epistemic justification, but they also created two significant and unavoidable problems. The first of these is that a normative assessment generally requires a foil, which is to say something against which to judge itself. A normative construction that simply posits who the stakeholders are and what their stakes are is axiomatic and is therefore easily refuted or rejected by equally axiomatic statements like, for example, "nuh-uh." Therefore, normative interpretations of stakeholder models must start from the presumption that they are responding to something that is, by definition, morally incorrect. And in a business sense, that "something" is invariably the same thing. Every time. As Donaldson and Preston put it, "One way to construct a normative foundation for the stakeholder model is to examine its principal competitor, the model of management control in the interests of shareowners, as represented by the business judgment rule."[20]

This is one of the central problems of stakeholder modeling and is, therefore, the subject of the entire next chapter.

In the meantime, the second problem with normative assessments of stakeholder models is that it necessitates choosing an ethical principle from which to launch the analysis. This, of course, is the problem already diagnosed with respect to the other fields of academic inquiry. In order to assess the morality of something, one must first define what is moral.

Stakeholder theory, like all academic social studies, is host to a variety of opinions and theories about morality and thus about which moral principles need to be elevated above all others, which ethical theories should guide the analysis, "such as individual or group 'rights,' 'social contract,' or utilitarianism."[21] In their original joint analysis, Edward Freeman and William Evan determined that the value that mattered most was "democratization" or "individual rights," or as Donaldson and Preston noted, "They asserted that the theory of the firm must be reconceptualized 'along essentially Kantian lines.' This means each stakeholder group has a right to be treated as an end in itself, and not as means to some other end, 'and therefore must participate in determining the future direction of the firm in which [it has] a stake.'"[22]

In this, you can see the not-so-subtle shifting of the ground away from the "instrumental" version of the stakeholder model, that which suggests that corporate managers should assess stakeholders in terms of the broader corporate goals. Almost immediately upon introducing a normative component to the discussion, Freeman moves explicitly and irreversibly away from the idea that this is about a corporation at all or about its success.

Predictably, when Freeman and Evan advocated a deontological normative treatment of the stakeholder idea, they played Pandora to the Epimetheus of American business. Once they had lifted the lid on their box, the entirety of the academy's ideological *daimones* escaped to wreak havoc on the planet, leaving the Titan of Hindsight regretting having accepted strategic planning's "gift" to him. As a result, there are utilitarian interpretations of stakeholder theory. There are feminist interpretations. There are integrative social contract interpretations. There are Critical Theory interpretations—because why wouldn't there be? Name an ethical system, and there is almost certainly an interpretation of stakeholder theory that utilizes it.

Probably the most common interpretation, however, is that which adopts a "pragmatic" approach to the ethics of stakeholder theory. Actually, according to Freeman, it's a "neopragmatic" approach, one he thinks fits his original work and subsequent reflection upon it most favorably.[23]

It is important to note here that the "pragmatism" involved in the broader stakeholder enterprise is not the pragmatism of what might be called "common sense." This is not pragmatism in the colloquial sense of the word. Remember, Edward Freeman is a philosopher by training, and his pragmatism is, therefore, a philosophical pragmatism, an approach to business strategy and the stakeholder "genre" that harnesses the ethical formulations of John Dewey, John Rawls, and Richard Rorty.

Of the three, Dewey likely is the most important, Rawls the best known, and Rorty the most controversial and most pernicious. For the purposes of this examination of the effects of this neopragmatism on stakeholder theory and then, by extension, on the politicization of capital markets, it might be helpful to look a little more closely at the ideas espoused by the two more important of the three, Rawls and Dewey. It would take an entire book—several, perhaps—to address either of these two in any detail, but there are portions of their work that are more relevant than others, broad ideas that are vitally important, given their impact on the stakeholder attack on free and fair capital markets.

In general, philosophical pragmatism has the same roots as colloquial pragmatism, that is to say that it is about practicality and results. Ideology is unimportant, even damaging, and the only thing that matters is arriving at the best possible outcome. Pragmatism insists that knowledge is fallible, that experience is incredibly useful, and that absolutism is the enemy of understanding.

Sounds nice, yes?

Well...no. Pragmatism is also a cliché-riddled mess, as Jonah Goldberg spent an entire book documenting.[24] Pragmatism is also the rejection of absolute truth; the dismissal of any sort of overarching metaphysical structure, including religion; and the denial of the distinction between ends and means. All that matters is results.

Pragmatism was the political approach taken by Barack Obama, who spent eight years lecturing the American people about how their stubborn clinging to moral and religious principles resulted in a series of "false choices." You don't have to choose between being good and being right, Obama would intone, echoing neopragmatist darling Richard Rorty. You just have to accept what I say, what I tell you will work. And if you do, you will be both good and right, because goodness, such as it is, derives from rightness.

Pragmatism has a long history in the United States, dating to the post–Civil War era, and it is one of the nation's few native philosophical traditions. Like all of the post-Enlightenment traditions, it rejects the tradition and the "superstition" of the old order and seeks to replace it with something more "rational," something based on reason, observation, and trial and error.

Although William James and Charles Sanders Pierce are generally credited with developing the idea, the American thinker most generally associated with pragmatism is John Dewey. Dewey was born and raised in Burlington, Vermont, graduated from the University of Vermont in 1879, and became an elementary school teacher. He taught for three years before deciding his true vocation lay elsewhere. He attended graduate school at and received his PhD from … wait for it … the brand-new Johns Hopkins University! Dewey was awarded his PhD in 1884, three years before Woodrow Wilson earned his, but Dewey's brother Davis was both a friend of Wilson's and a student of Richard Ely's, which is to say that John Dewey swam in the same intellectual waters as the other early heroes of American Progressivism. Among those under whom Dewey studied while at Hopkins was the aforementioned Charles Sanders Pierce, from whom he gained his appreciation for pragmatism.

After teaching for a few years at the University of Michigan, Dewey went to teach at the also brand-new University of Chicago, which, like Hopkins, was designed to have a German-inspired graduate program focused on new and innovative research. In 1904, Dewey resettled at Columbia University, and in 1919 was one of the founders of The New School.

At the time, and for a great while afterward, Dewey was seen by many as *the* American philosopher, the only thinker who really mattered. Today, however, Dewey is best known as a pioneer in education.

Dewey considered himself neither a Marxist nor a Socialist of any sort. And yet he—in conjunction with his tireless promoter Sidney Hook—probably did more to inculcate Americans with post-Enlightenment leftism than any other person. Like Mill and Kant and Hume and the rest who came before him, Dewey disdained the idea of an existing body of acquired human social and moral knowledge that could and should be passed down from generation to generation in the form of custom and tradition. He believed that knowledge was not something that could be learned but something every individual student had to discover for himself. Dewey was dogmatic about this. He denigrated the traditional practice of focusing on teaching such subjects as reading, writing, mathematics, and history, and promoted the teaching of social and "thinking" skills instead. This, he thought, would be the salvation of mankind, learning to think without preconceptions.

Dewey was obsessed with the idea of "critical thinking," or, as he preferred to call it, "reflective thinking." The key to Dewey's pragmatism was the belief in the idea that man should not be taught knowledge, but, rather, should be taught how to attain knowledge on his own. "There will be almost a revolution in school education," he wrote, "when study and learning are treated not as acquisition of what others know but as development of capital to be invested in eager alertness in observing and judging the conditions under which one lives."[25]

Dewey's fixation on reflective thinking is significant in this context for two reasons. First, as noted above, Dewey's pragmatism hinged on the notion that the existing social and moral structure was an inadequate guide to making decisions, moral decisions chief among them. The pragmatist, he believed, must discard all the knowledge and tradition of his forefathers and discover it anew, on his own and without the conditions imposed by large ideological and moral structures.

Second, while critical thinking and Critical Theory are not necessarily related, they both sprang from a common ancestor, that which the French philosopher Paul Ricoeur called the "hermeneutics of suspicion," and which the aforementioned American intellectual Roger Kimball called "the hermeneutics of contempt."[26] The American literary theorist Rita Felski described the hermeneutics of suspicion as a "common spirit that pervades the writings of Marx, Freud, and Nietzsche." Despite their obvious differences, Felski argued, these thinkers jointly constitute a "school of suspicion." That is to say, they share a commitment to unmasking "the lies and illusions of consciousness; they are the architects of a distinctively modern style of interpretation that circumvents obvious or self-evident meanings in order to draw out less visible and less flattering truths."[27]

This clearly describes both the critical theorists of the Frankfurt School and the critical thinkers of the Deweyan pragmatist school. And the end result of both schools, unrelated though their techniques may be, is that which Kimball noted "is not criticism but what one wit called 'criticismism': the 'ism' or ideology of being critical."[28]

The relevance here should be clear. For nearly an entire century now, American students have been encouraged to see themselves as the linchpin in the accumulation of knowledge. They have been taught to treat everything they absorb with disdain and to believe that their own "truth," their own solutions, are superior to anything that anyone else may tell them. They have been encouraged to favor antagonism and deconstruction over constructive engagement, to view everything they see, read, and come into contact with critically. American students are taught—specifically and intentionally—to look for flaws and inconsistencies and to tear down rather than build up. In short, because of the "pragmatist" interpretation of "critical thinking," all Americans are taught to be critical of everything and to presume that every existing bit of information they see is wrong, biased, or prejudiced.

And because of the focus on pragmatist ethics in stakeholder theory, all of this now applies to American corporations as well.

As for John Rawls, until fairly recently his connection to ideological pragmatism was considered tenuous. Over the last two decades, however, that connection has been bolstered both theoretically and with the discovery of unpublished writings. In any case Freeman, alone and in conjunction with William Evan, uses Rawls and his theory of justice to develop the broader stakeholder understanding of corporations.

For many on the Left, the turning point in the battle for control of the hearts and minds of the people and the battle for the soul of liberty came in 1971 with the publication of John Rawls's *A Theory of Justice*. Before the publication of this book, Rawls was largely unknown outside of the provincial world of moral philosophy; he was an average and modestly successful philosopher, whatever that means. After his *Theory*, however, Rawls became a global superstar and among the most prominent voices in public morality in the West. When he presented Rawls with the National Humanities Medal in 1999, Bill Clinton declared emphatically that the philosopher's work had "helped a whole generation of learned Americans revive their faith in democracy itself." And indeed, as much as anyone, Rawls has been the inspiration for the "learned"—which is to say the liberal Left—for nearly the past half-century.

Put simply, Rawls's theory of justice is based on two principles, which he spells out as follows:

First Principle: Each person has the same indefeasible claim to a fully adequate scheme of equal basic liberties, which scheme is compatible with the same scheme of liberties for all;

Second Principle: Social and economic inequalities are to satisfy two conditions:

They are to be attached to offices and positions open to all under conditions of *fair equality of opportunity*;

They are to be to the greatest benefit of the least-advantaged members of society (the *difference principle*).[29]

Here, Rawls's "expanded" social contract blends both negative rights (the First Principle) and the supposition of positive rights (the Second Principle). The First Principle dictates the minimum liberty afforded to all members of society, while the Second stipulates that justice can only be achieved if all are provided the same opportunity, including the same economic opportunity. Hence, a "just" society demands economic redistribution.

Rawls intended for these principles to be lexically arranged, which is to say that the First must be met before the Second can be considered. In practice, however, since all basic liberties must be equally accessible to all, even the First Principle demands some measure of redistribution of wealth. Moreover, Rawls argued explicitly against a right to unlimited "private property," which is to say that he believes that, even in a nominally capitalist society, wealth, resources, and access to opportunity must be fairly distributed. Arguing against what he called "welfare-state capitalism" and in favor of a "property-owing democracy," Rawls claimed that the former "permits a small class to have a near-monopoly of the means of production," while the latter "avoids this, not by the redistribution of income to those with less at the end of each period, so to speak, but rather by ensuring the widespread ownership of assets and human capital (that is, education and trained skills) at the beginning of each period, all this against a background of fair equality of opportunity." Therefore the point—of government or of any justice-seeking institution—"is not simply to assist those who lose out through accident or misfortune (although that must be done), but rather to put all citizens in a position to manage their own affairs on a footing of a suitable degree of social and economic equality."[30]

In many ways, Rawls and his theory of justice allowed the contemporary Left to embrace its fetishization of positive liberty. He squared the circle left by Rousseau, conceding the necessity of basic negative rights but emphasizing the moral requirement of positive rights as well. He provided the best of both worlds and thereby offered what the Left has seen ever since as a plausibly ethical political platform, limited acknowledgment of individual liberty coupled with a far less limited demand for economically just institutions.

Not coincidentally, Rawls also squared the circle for the aforementioned pragmatist Barack Obama, who famously complained that the

Constitution is "a charter of negative liberties. It says what the states can't do to you. Says what the federal government can't do to you but doesn't say what the federal government or state government must do on your behalf."[31] Rawls provided a theory of justice that made redistributionism seem fair and, indeed, necessary.

By the end of the twentieth century, the idea of stakeholder analysis or stakeholder planning or the stakeholder "genre," as its most prominent theorist called it, had become almost indistinguishable from any of the other tools in the "social science" world. Though housed in a different part of the academy than philosophy, economics, sociology, psychology, public administration, and the rest, the strategic planning and ethics functions of business education had been just as thoroughly stripped of their practicality. Making matters worse, because most business educators and students still generally considered themselves more levelheaded and functional than their social science peers, and because stakeholder analysis had evolved from procedures that were utilized by businesses to improve their function in real-world cases, the collapse of the strategic stakeholder genre into moralistic mush went at least partially unacknowledged, leaving the business world frightfully unprepared for what would come next.

CHAPTER 5

FRIEDMAN, SOREL, AND THE HEROIC MYTH

For the better part of a century, the forces of the political and intellectual Left slowly, carefully, purposefully wound their way through the Western cultural landscape and the American political and educational landscapes to arrive at a point of denouement. For most of the institutions of American society, that denouement came in the late 1960s and early 1970s, when the strength and intensity of the "counterculture" eclipsed that of the traditional culture. As detailed above, the streams connected during this era, creating a vast, rushing wave of cultural, educational, and political change.

Without intending to apply the label "reactionary," which is now little more than an epithet meant to demonize any and all resistance to radicalism, the Left's long march did not proceed without obstructions. On occasion, serious and smart but largely isolated forces defied the radicalization of the entirety of the culture. Some of this resistance was overtly conservative: "Slow down." "You're bowdlerizing 2,000 years of history and 200 years of community." "Think about what you're doing before you do it." And so on.

Much of it, however, was not explicitly conservative but was, rather, purely intellectual. The critiques were aimed not at the impulsiveness or sloppiness of the march through the institutions, but at the accuracy and validity of the scholarship and the actions it invited. This case was not one of concern for propriety but one of concern for veracity. You're not just being careless, the response went, you're also producing poor results.

You're wrong *on the facts*. Your efforts are in contravention of objective truth and are thus not instructive but destructive.

In the area of public management and administration, such luminaries as Theodore Lowi—a future president of both the American Political Science Association and the International Political Science Association—knocked the advance of the administrative state for its delegation of responsibility to unelected and thus unaccountable entities, which then built their own power bases, often in conflict with the will of the American people.[1] Gordon Tullock, then an international economics instructor at the University of South Carolina, identified the "rent-seeking" and "regulatory capture" features of the federal bureaucracy in 1967,[2] while Anne Krueger, an economist at the University of Minnesota, confirmed the hypothesis and the concept seven years later.[3] William Niskanen identified the "budget-maximizing" behavior of bureaucracy in 1968, the same year that Dwight Waldo was busy telling young bureaucrats-in-training to go out to all the world and apply their values to the administration of the people's government.[4]

In the broader realm of the "social sciences," throughout the entire decade of the 1960s, Karl Popper, Hans Albert, and the critical rationalists duked it out with Theodor Adorno, Jurgen Habermas, Herbert Marcuse, and the Critical Theorists of the Frankfurt School. The debate—mistakenly labeled the "positivism dispute," despite the fact that both sides were antipositivist—essentially hinged on whether political actions based on social science should also be based on reality or on metareality instead. And while Popper didn't identify the targets of his musings, one may infer, given the timing and content of them, that he had Adorno and the Critical Theorists in mind when he offered his "conspiracy theory of society." "This theory," Popper began, "which is more primitive than most forms of theism, is akin to Homer's theory of society. Homer conceived the power of the gods in such a way that whatever happened on the plain before Troy was only a reflection of the various conspiracies on Olympus. The conspiracy theory of society is just a version of this theism, of a belief in gods whose whims and wills rule everything. It comes from abandoning God and then asking: 'Who is in his place?'"[5]

But of all the resistance efforts, one stood out above all the rest. Interestingly, it was a preemptive effort, one born of foresight rather than reaction. The September 13, 1970 edition of the *New York Times*

Magazine contained an op-ed written by a monetarist economist from the University of Chicago, who would go on to win the Nobel Prize in Economics six years later. His name was Milton Friedman, and the ideas he discussed in the op-ed would form the foundation of what would come to be known as "the Friedman Doctrine" or the "shareholder theory of capitalism." Friedman was practiced at the art of explaining serious economic matters to a popular audience, having written a weekly economics column for *Newsweek* magazine for the previous four years. What he wrote for the *Times* was simple, clear, and exceptionally powerful. As such, it is worth quoting at length:

> In a free-enterprise, private-property system, a corporate executive is an employee of the owners of the business. He has direct responsibility to his employers. That responsibility is to conduct the business in accordance with their desires, which generally will be to make as much money as possible while conforming to the basic rules of the society, both those embodied in law and those embodied in ethical custom. Of course, in some cases his employers may have a different objective. A group of persons might establish a corporation for an eleemosynary purpose, for example, a hospital or a school. The manager of such a corporation will not have money profit as his objective but the rendering of certain services.
>
> In either case, the key point is that, in his capacity as a corporate executive, the manager is the agent of the individuals who own the corporation or establish the eleemosynary institution, and his primary responsibility is to them.
>
> Needless to say, this does not mean that it is easy to judge how well he is performing his task. But at least the criterion of performance is straightforward, and the persons among whom a voluntary contractual arrangement exists are clearly defined.
>
> Of course, the corporate executive is also a person in his own right. As a person, he may have many other responsibilities that he recognizes or assumes voluntarily—to his family, his conscience, his feelings of charity, his church, his clubs, his city, his country. He may feel impelled by these responsibilities to devote part of his income to causes he regards as worthy, to refuse to work for particular corporations, even to leave his job, for example, to join his country's armed forces.

If we wish, we may refer to some of these responsibilities as "social responsibilities." But in these respects he is acting as a principal, not an agent; he is spending his own money or time or energy, not the money of his employers or the time or energy he has contracted to devote to their purposes. If these are "social responsibilities," they are the social responsibilities of individuals, not of business.

What does it mean to say that the corporate executive has a "social responsibility" in his capacity as businessman? If this statement is not pure rhetoric, it must mean that he is to act in some way that is not in the interest of his employers. For example, that he is to refrain from increasing the price of the product in order to contribute to the social objective of preventing inflation, even though a price increase would be in the best interests of the corporation. Or that he is to make expenditures on reducing pollution beyond the amount that is in the best interests of the corporation or that is required by law in order to contribute to the social objective of improving the environment. Or that, at the expense of corporate profits, he is to hire "hardcore" unemployed instead of better qualified available workmen to contribute to the social objective of reducing poverty.

In each of these cases, the corporate executive would be spending someone else's money for a general social interest. Insofar as his actions in accord with his "social responsibility" reduce returns to stockholders, he is spending their money. Insofar as his actions raise the price to customers, he is spending the customers' money. Insofar as his actions lower the wages of some employees, he is spending their money.

The stockholders or the customers or the employees could separately spend their own money on the particular action if they wished to do so. The executive is exercising a distinct "social responsibility," rather than serving as an agent of the stockholders or the customers or the employees, only if he spends the money in a different way than they would have spent it.[6]

The doctrine spelled out in these paragraphs has been both wildly popular and wildly ridiculed. It is the subject of continuous discussion and continuous criticism. Much of what it actually says is ignored by critics, and much of what critics say it includes, it does not. Most of the discussion about the doctrine is best addressed in the context of that criticism, but at least a couple of broad generalizations may be made first. For starters, this is a purely normative document. It is not about procedures or actions or techniques or models. It is about the simple ethical proposition that if one agrees to work for a company, one also agrees that the performance of his professional duties will be carried out in the best interests of the company. That interest will generally be to make as much money as possible, but not always, and will only be within "*the basic rules of the society, both those embodied in law and those embodied in ethical custom.*"

Additionally, because this doctrine is purely prescriptive—i.e., asserting and explaining a moral responsibility—it is in no way descriptive, which is to say that Friedman does not presume to tell anyone anywhere how to best go about conducting the business of making money. He does not suggest that managers should screw over their workers. He does not suggest that managers should ignore the environment. He does not suggest that employees should stick it to the customer. He doesn't even offer a time horizon in which the managers' responsibilities should be conducted. He doesn't say they need to meet quarterly guidance or annual goals or any other metric, for that matter. All he says is that the managers of the corporation should do what is in the best interests of the corporation and its shareholders. Whatever that means and however that is accomplished are not Friedman's concerns (as long as it all follows the "basic rules of the society").

What this suggests is that the clash between stakeholders and shareholders is a false dichotomy. Indeed, since stakeholder theory is derived from the efforts to improve company performance over a longer event horizon, it is quite clear that any conflict between the two is related to new variables added to the equation after the rules were written, meaning that the idea that stakeholders and shareholders are necessarily antagonistic is a fiction added post hoc to justify the ongoing development of an academic exercise. The normative shareholder model would be perfectly compatible with a literally endless number of descriptive or instrumental stakeholder models. It is only the desire to substitute a different normative system or goal that brings shareholders and stakeholders into conflict. It is a purely exogenous distinction.

The most prominent critique of the Friedman Doctrine is that it gets the relationship between shareholders and the company wrong. The "agency theory," which, as Friedman puts it, means that "as a corporate executive, the manager is the agent of the individuals who own the corporation." As Joseph Bower and Lynn Paine famously noted, "From a legal perspective, shareholders are beneficiaries of the corporation's activities, but they do not have 'dominion' over a piece of property. Nor do they enjoy access to the corporate premises or use of the corporation's assets. What shareholders do own is their shares."[7] This is an important distinction and one that should not be glossed over. The corporate executive simply does not work directly for the shareholders but for the "firm."

Additionally, it is impossible to treat hundreds, thousands, or millions of shareholders as a single "owner." Again, as Bower and Paine put it, "Shareholders have differing investment objectives, attitudes toward risk, and time horizons." This, too, is an important point. Agency theory and Friedman's explication of it have some flaws that cannot be overlooked.

At the same time, most of the problems associated with the agency model are problems not with Friedman's description of it but with additions that were added later. For example, Bower and Paine state that "agency theory's recommended alignment between managers' interests and those of shareholders can skew the perspective of the entire organization. When the interests of successive layers of management are 'aligned' in this manner, the corporation may become so biased toward the narrow interests of its current shareholders that it fails to meet the requirements of its customers or other constituencies." That's a fair and important point, but it has nothing to do with Friedman or with the basic shareholder theory he set forth. The "alignment" portion of the idea was added six years later by Michael Jensen and William Meckling in their seminal article "Theory of the Firm: Managerial Behavior, Agency Costs and Ownership Structure."[8] And even then, it was another 14 years before Michael Jensen and Kevin Murphy introduced the idea of paying corporate executives according to performance and ensuring that they were "invested" in that performance as significant shareholders.[9]

A second prominent critique of the shareholder model is that placing too much emphasis on "shareholder value" is an enormous mistake that causes short-term thinking, financialization of companies, and failure to innovate and plan for the long term. In his 2018 book *The Age of Agile*, Steve Denning, the former program director in Knowledge Management at the World Bank, collected quotes from a veritable Who's Who of corporate managers decrying the "shareholder value" idea. For example, Jack Welch, the former CEO of General Electric and a management guru, called the shareholder value theory "the dumbest idea in the world." Vinci Group Chairman and CEO Xavier Huillard called shareholder value theory "totally idiotic." Paul Polman, CEO of Unilever, decried "the cult of shareholder value."[10] And so on.

What Denning fails to mention is that this "shareholder value" notion is not a part of Milton Friedman's original idea. Rather, it was one of the contributions to management theory made by one of the corporate executives Denning quoted deriding it. As the *Financial Times* noted upon Jack Welch's retirement, "[t]he birth of the shareholder value movement is commonly traced to a speech that Mr. Welch gave at New York's Pierre hotel in 1981, shortly after taking the helm at GE."[11]

The problem with conflating the "shareholder" model of a corporation with the "shareholder value" theory is that it imputes to Friedman ideas that he did not state or against which he hedged. Friedman did not say, for example, that the corporate manager had a responsibility to maximize share price. He said the manager has a responsibility "to conduct the business in accordance with their [the shareholders'] desires, which generally will be to make as much money as possible." His explicit aim—to make as much money as possible—is not identical to increasing share price or shareholder "value." As the financialization of the last twelve years has shown, it is perfectly possible to increase shareholder value and share price without making money.

Additionally, it's clear that Friedman hedges himself for a reason, conceding that shareholders' interests will not always correlate with making as much money as possible. Since his is a normative argument, Friedman is careful to leave room for the possibility that shareholders may, at some point, under some conditions, have a legitimate reason not to want their corporate manager to make as much money as possible. The absolutism ascribed to Friedman by his critics is, quite simply, misplaced.

The confusion here almost certainly springs from the confusion between what Friedman's model is and how later iterations differed from his. Recall that Friedman's model is purely normative. It does not dabble in the details of how to achieve that normative end. The Jensen and Meckling model, by contrast, is descriptive, e.g., "We define the concept of agency costs, show its relationship to the 'separation and control' issue, investigate the nature of the agency costs generated by the existence of debt and outside equity, demonstrate who bears the costs and why, and investigate the Pareto optimality of their existence."[12] Likewise, Jensen and Murphy's take on shareholder theory is instrumental, e.g., "CEOs should own substantial amounts of company stock....Cash compensation should be structured to provide big rewards for outstanding performance and meaningful penalties for poor performance....Make real the threat of dismissal."[13]

Those who criticize the "shareholder" model of democracy often make very serious and very important criticisms of policies associated with the idea that a corporation exists to make money. Too often, however, those critiques have nothing whatsoever to do with the underlying normative theory outlined by Friedman. Rather, they are more properly directed at the descriptive and instrumental applications of the theory. They are not arguments against "shareholder" primacy at all, but against some of the less sensible implementations of the idea.

But if this is the case, then why, exactly, do Friedman's critics continue to conflate his normative case with the instrumental application of it? Surely, they know better. So why do they not correct their errors and the historical record?

The short answer to these questions is because it serves their purposes. The longer and more complicated answer probably has at least three parts, two of which derive in large part from the nature of the criticisms offered.

Recall that those who created the normative approach to stakeholder analysis found it easier to state and to justify their ethical positions when they were able to do so in contrast to an existing ethical position. As Donaldson and Preston put it, "One way to construct a normative foundation for the stakeholder model is to examine its principal competitor, the model of management control in the interests of shareowners, as represented by the business judgment rule."[14]

The business judgment rule is not the same thing as the Friedman Doctrine or the basic normative shareholder model, but the point stands nonetheless. It is easier to create a normative model of stakeholder interest if there is something to contrast it against, if there is a foil against which the new model can appear to be fairer and more just.

That leads right into the second reason that the shareholder model is so roundly and thoroughly attacked, namely that it's easy to caricature and thus to demonize. The beauty in what Friedman laid out is that it is simple. If you work for the company, then your obligation, as an employee of the company, is to advance the interests of the company, generally measured in terms of making the most money. Unfortunately, because it is so simple, it is also easy to lampoon—and to vilify.

"Pick the target," Saul Alinsky wrote, "freeze it, personalize it, and polarize it."[15] Have you ever in your life seen the stakeholder model referred to as "the Freeman model"? Of course you haven't. Conversely, have you ever seen the shareholder model discussed when it *wasn't* referred to as the Friedman Doctrine or at least tied to Friedman in some conspicuous way? Again, of course not. The aforementioned Steve Denning, writing at Forbes in 2017, declared that "When shareholder value was first put forward by Milton Friedman in 1970, [Joseph] Bower, then a young associate professor at Harvard Business School, was interviewed by National Public Radio. He told NPR that maximizing shareholder value as the sole goal of business was 'pernicious nonsense.'"[16] But then, as noted above, "shareholder value" is not what Friedman put forward. It is close to what he put forward and may be derived in later iterations from what he put forward, but it's not the same thing. But because Friedman is easily caricatured as a one-dimensional figure, and because his theory is simple enough that it, too, can be caricatured as one-dimensional—i.e., it's all about the money—they have been targeted, frozen, personalized, and polarized.

The final reason that Friedman and his model are so easily and frequently attacked—which is related to the first and the second reasons—is because it is "pragmatic" to do so.

Among the great pantheon of pragmatic thinkers, there are a few whom most pragmatists would prefer not to discuss in any great detail, one of whom was a French engineer named Georges Sorel. Throughout his three decades as a radical and a writer, Sorel embraced an eclectic mix of Marxist and other Leftist thought. He supported the revolution, advocated for violence, and yet feared the collapse of Christianity and the rise of the omnipotent state in its place. More than anything, in his early writings, Sorel was a syndicalist, which is to say that he was a supporter of small, worker-based revolutionary groups that sought to change the relationship between labor and capital through either the use or the threat of violence and strikes.

Sorel is probably best known for his ideas about how best to create the conditions that he and the workers sought. Sorel described the fundamentals of a revolutionary movement that could convincingly wield the threat of a violent "general strike," which, he believed, could bring all production to a halt and result in the takeover of the means of production.

But Sorel wasn't necessarily interested in a general strike, per se, which might be complicated and unpredictable. Rather, he was more interested in the *idea* of a general strike, in a glorious "myth" of the general strike, which would motivate workers to action and strike fear into the hearts of capitalists. The strike didn't actually need to happen. It only needed to attract heroes to the cause and inspire their glorious deeds.

Sorel's theory of revolution, and particularly his premise of the glorious myth, became one of the most important weapons in the Leftist arsenal from that point on. Sorel argued that the creation and promotion of myths was much more persuasive in motivating people than truth, reason, economic theories, or obtuse philosophical discussions. Indeed, he argued that workers grasp myths intuitively, which, in turn, meant that there was no need for a Leninist élite schooled in the scientific theory of Marxism and no need for or benefit from an all-powerful state. Real strikes were financially and personally damaging. They were, in many cases, disastrous for the men and women involved. But the myth...the myth could only make heroes.

Sorel also insisted that all of the great events and movements of history were driven by these myths, including Christianity, which he claimed was the most successful utilization of the heroic myth in all of human history.

As with many of the Leftist thinkers of the early twentieth century, Sorel's plans, dreams, and expectations were interrupted and undercut by World War I. Nevertheless, in 1921 he published his final major work, the work that cemented his conversion to full-fledged pragmatism: the fittingly titled *De l'Utilité du Pragmatisme* (*On the Utility of Pragmatism*). And while Sorel didn't discuss the glorious myth in his final turn to pragmatism, it is nevertheless clear that the myth, in its original construction, was pragmatic in its nature. The myth replaces the need for revolution. It replaces the need for death, violence, and destruction and replaces them with the *threat* of death, violence, and destruction, with the *myth* of death, violence, and destruction. The myth does not need to be realized. It only needs to be believed and for that belief to produce better ends. "Even if the only result of the myth is to render the socialist conception more heroic," Sorel wrote, "it already would on that account alone be looked upon as having incalculable value."[17]

In the context of advancing the stakeholder theory of the corporation, it doesn't matter one whit what Milton Friedman actually said. It doesn't matter that his model is normative and not descriptive or instrumental. It doesn't matter that his notion of shareholder supremacy is perfectly compatible with any number of stakeholder plans. It doesn't matter that he didn't push the "shareholder value" proposition, that he didn't say that it was important to align management interests with shareholder interests by making managers minority owners of the company, that he didn't promote the greed or the venality that came to be associated with capital markets in the 1980s, that he didn't say that quarterly results were the standards by which executives should be judged. None of this matters at all. The only thing that matters is the myth of Friedman, the myth of the greedy shareholder and the rapacious capitalists, the myth that shareholders and stakeholders must, always and everywhere, be opposed to one another.

Milton Friedman's 1970 defense of shareholders stands as one of the most impressive and influential works of economics, popular or otherwise, in the last one hundred years, at least. It is not a perfect defense, obviously, and does, indeed, raise questions about agency and ownership.

At the same time, it is also not a doctrine that promotes greed, selfishness, financialization, or the subjugation of stakeholders to a tyranny of shareholders. That is a myth, but it is a myth that was intentionally cultivated and perfidiously applied to advance normative—which is to say ethical or moral—ends. These ends almost certainly would otherwise not have seemed as necessary, benign, or profitable.

The creation and promotion of the myth was, in many ways, the reactionary position in the intellectual development of business management. When Friedman wrote his shareholder piece, he was addressing the general social, political, and educational milieu, which was churning under the pressure applied by the two great streams of cultural Leftism. The mythmakers, for all their effort, have not yet been able to displace

Friedman's simple normative calculus, but they continue to try. His "theory" and the business world's acceptance of it have thus far preserved American industry, the last standing cultural institution, from falling to the long march. But a new myth has taken hold, at least in the halls of academia. And the struggle continues, generation by generation, as befits the long war.

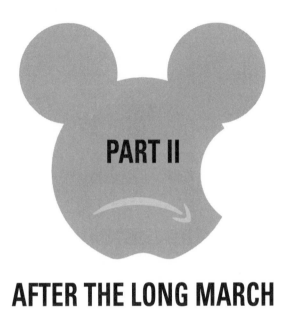

PART II

AFTER THE LONG MARCH

CHAPTER 6

FROM SRI TO ESG

There is no small irony in the fact that the idea of "socially responsible investing" likely has its philosophical roots in the theology of John Wesley. Historically, Wesley is very much the "anti-Calvin," which is to say that his theology was deeply influenced by John Calvin, many of whose reform precepts Wesley studied, considered, and rejected. Calvin, of course, was the progenitor of modern capitalism—at least if Max Weber can be believed. Calvin's conception of predestination, and the related belief that material wealth and economic success are the outward signs of God's favor, gave rise to the "Protestant work ethic," which, in turn, gave rise to the "spirit of capitalism."

Wesley, for his part, saw three Christian obligations with respect to money: to gain as much as you can; to save as much as you can; and to give as much as you can. In keeping with the first and second of these obligations, however, Wesley instructed his followers to be leery about the means by which they earned and saved. In his famous sermon "The Use of Money," Wesley stipulated the following:

> [M]oney should be regarded as a gift of God for the benefits that it brings in ordering the affairs of civilization and the opportunities it offers for doing good. In the hands of God's children, money is food for the hungry, clothing for the naked and shelter for the stranger. With money we can care for the widow and the fatherless, defend the oppressed, meet the need of those who are sick or in pain....

We should not gain money at the expense of life or health. No sum of money, however large, should induce us to accept employment which would injure our bodies. Neither should we begin (or continue in) any business which deprives us of the food and sleep that we need. We may draw a distinction between businesses which are absolutely unhealthy, such as those that deal directly with dangerous materials, and those employments which would be harmful to those of a weak constitution....

The rule is further limited by the necessity not to undertake any employment which might injure our minds. This includes the pursuit of any trade which is against the law of God or the law of the land. It is just as wrong to defraud the king of taxes as it is to steal from our fellow citizens. There are businesses which might be innocent in themselves but which, at least in England at this time require cheating, lying or other customs which are contrary to good conscience, to provide an adequate income. These, too, we should avoid.[1]

The modern version of socially responsible investing has many parents, including Phillip Carret, the longtime value investor and friend of Warren Buffett. Carret started his mutual fund—which would become the Pioneer Fund—in 1928, avoiding investments in companies that produced alcohol or tobacco. Carret was not alone, however; throughout the 1950s and early 1960s, various religious groups also began limiting their investments to avoid "sin stocks."

In 1971, with the launch of the Pax World Balanced Fund, socially responsible investment began to gain some serious, if still fringe, momentum. Unsurprisingly, this momentum came courtesy of two United Methodist ministers, Luther Tyson and Jack Corbett, who were opposed to the Vietnam War and wanted, therefore, to avoid having church investments placed in any company that might be associated with "war profiteering."[2] Pax was followed very closely by the First Spectrum Fund, which promised that it would screen companies for performance in "the environment, civil rights and the protection of consumers."[3]

By the early 1980s, socially responsible investment was common, was standardized, and was mostly a politically and socially conservative approach to investing. Standard screens avoided alcohol, tobacco, weapons, gambling, and pornography and appealed mostly to religious investors, especially conservative religious investors.

All of that began to change, however, in 1984, with the Union Carbide disaster in Bhopal, India. After Bhopal, more investors on the political Left—those concerned primarily with the environment—also became more interested and involved in socially responsible investing. That same year, the United States Social Investment Forum (now called the Sustainable and Responsible Investment Forum) was launched as a clearinghouse of information to help investors find investments that suited their specific ethical concerns.

Around the same time, a new form of socially responsible investment started developing on some of the nation's largest and most respected college campuses. Protests against the white minority apartheid regime in South Africa evolved to take on a financial component, one that eventually helped end apartheid and make Nobel Peace Prize winners out of the unlikeliest pair.

In 1948, the Afrikaner National Party won control of the South African government and immediately began enforcing old segregation laws and enacting new ones. In 1961, the party withdrew South Africa from the British Commonwealth and declared it an independent republic, expanding and strengthening the "apartheid" laws. During the 1950s the African National Congress (ANC), which was comprised mostly of black South Africans, began to resist the apartheid regime. In 1960, in the black township of Sharpsville, white police attempted to disperse a crowd that was protesting without a permit and opened fire, killing 67 people and wounding almost 200 more. From that moment on, the National Party and its apartheid regime became global pariahs.

In 1963, the apartheid government had ANC leader Nelson Mandela arrested and imprisoned. Ten years later the United Nations officially condemned apartheid, and then, three years after that, placed an arms embargo on the regime. In 1985, both the United States and the United Kingdom imposed severe economic sanctions on South Africa, hoping to bring an end to apartheid and the increasingly violent protests against it.

For all the efforts of the world's most powerful nations and its most august international organizations, the tactic that finally got through to the regime and forced it to blink was one created at the grassroots level, harnessing the power of shareholders.

In the mid-1970s, Leon Sullivan, a civil rights leader and a Baptist minister in Philadelphia, who also happened to be a director on the board of General Motors, became interested in and concerned about the protest movement targeting South Africa. Sullivan abhorred the apartheid government but also knew that economic sanctions, United Nations condemnations, and all the usual means of challenging rogue regimes would likely do more harm than good. He knew, for example, that GM was the single largest employer of black South Africans, which meant that sanctioning the company for doing business with the apartheid regime or forcing it to abandon the country altogether would also devastate precisely the people he and the other protesters hoped to help.

In 1977, Sullivan drafted a document that came, fittingly enough, to be called "The Sullivan Principles." It asked that companies who did business in South Africa abide by certain guidelines and behaviors, including a promise to be fair and equitable with its employees. Sullivan hoped that this fair and equitable corporate behavior would unsettle the racial dynamics in the factories. From there, the chaos could have ripple effects throughout the country. "Starting with the workplace," Sullivan said, "I tightened the screws step by step and raised the bar step by step. Eventually I got to the point where I said that companies must practice corporate civil disobedience against the laws, and I threatened South Africa and said in two years Mandela must be freed, apartheid must end, and blacks must vote, or else I'll bring every American company I can out of South Africa."[4]

Sullivan's principles didn't exactly work the way he'd hoped they would, but they laid the groundwork for a new category of socially responsible investing and a new tool to accomplish it. Sullivan and those who followed after him created a socially responsible investing strategy that was active, rather than passive. Rather than simply buying or selling shares of companies whose practices they favored or disfavored, the new socially responsible investor would use the clout granted to him as a shareholder—or the proxy for a large group of shareholders—to pressure companies to change their behavior to accommodate social or political ends. Sullivan's principles created the idea of "reputational risk," which could be used to pressure companies and to make a plausible case that their failure to act would hurt their business.

That same year, 1977, Hampshire College in Amherst, Massachusetts, took another huge step, turning the threat of shareholder action into reality, when its trustees agreed to divest its entire endowment from companies that did business in South Africa. The following year, Michigan State University followed suit, choosing total divestiture, and Columbia University and the University of Wisconsin chose to divest "selectively."

Because South African mineral resources were such an important part of the global economy at the time (accounting for up to 50 percent of the world's gold production),[5] a great many American companies did business in or with the apartheid regime, despite its odiousness. It is estimated that, in the early 1980s, somewhere between one-third and one-half of the S&P 500 had significant business dealings with South Africa.[6] Forcing these companies to end their relationships with the apartheid regime would cost them dearly. And that, of course, was the point. Fix South Africa; convince President Botha to end apartheid; use your economic power to produce change; or face the consequences.

By the end of the 1980s, some 155 colleges and universities had voted to divest from South Africa, while ninety cities, twenty-two counties, and twenty-six states had also become involved, enacting some form of economic rebuke to the regime. And this, in turn, meant that a significant number of public-employee pension funds were involved in divestiture as well.[7]

In 1989, National Party leader and South African President P. W. Botha suffered a stroke and was forced to resign. F. W. de Klerk, who had long since read the social, political, and especially economic handwriting on the wall, took leadership of the National Party and of the country and almost immediately set about ending the economic damage done by the divestment movement. De Klerk freed Nelson Mandela from prison, negotiated with the ANC to end minority rule, and dismantled the apartheid system as quickly as he could. Obviously, the divestment movement was not the only factor in ending apartheid, but just as obviously, it *did* play an outsized role. And in so doing, it fully inaugurated the new era in social investing—the era of shareholder activism.

At about that same time, in 1990, the Domini 400 Social Index was launched. It was the very first index designed to provide socially responsible investors access to primarily large-cap American companies, all of which met specific social, political, or environmental criteria.

Also in the early 1990s, Suzanne Harvey, a smart and ambitious staffer in the Washington research office of Prudential Securities, partnered with her boss, Mark Melcher, the famously conservative managing director of the office, to pitch a new social investment tool to the company's top brass. With their approval, she would create a research project within the Washington research team, dedicated to social investing. Management consented reluctantly, and Ms. Harvey soon launched the Social Investment Research Service (SIRS), which produced reports and screens on a whole host of social, political, and environmental issues. Users of the new service included both liberals and conservatives. Issues of concern ranged from the environment, women's issues, labor relations, abortion, the treatment of laboratory animals, and pornography to compliance with the Arab boycott of Israel. While SIRS mostly used the time-tested social screening methodology, avoiding the shareholder activism of the South Africa divestment campaign, the Service nevertheless represented a significant development in socially responsible investing. It was the first analyst team in a major institutional research department dedicated specifically to social investments.

SIRS became important for another reason as well. In 2000, as Prudential Securities was undergoing a series of management changes related to its parent company's demutualization, management trimmed the firm's macro-research budget and staffing. Among the analysts/ research groups cut were Suzanne Harvey and SIRS. At the time, Prudential Securities was in the habit of giving analysts it had fired the intellectual property rights to the work they'd done and the models they'd created. What this meant was that Ms. Harvey walked away from the firm with the name Social Investment Research Service and all of the investment screens she and her team had created. She then sold the name and the screens to Thompson Financial, where she became the first managing director of SIRS in the Thompson-owned operation called Institutional Shareholder Services (ISS). Suzanne didn't stay long at Thompson, but then, neither did ISS, which was sold to a group led by Warburg Pincus, then MSCI, which sold the group to Vestar Capital Partners, which, in turn, sold it in 2017 to its current owner, Genstar Capital, a private equity group from San Francisco.[8]

As ISS passed through successive owners it focused, at least publicly, on its main business, proxy advisory services. It kept SIRS, however, and, as will become clear later in this book, turned the operation into a massive and massively successful part of the ESG movement.

After the turn of the new century, the socially responsible investment idea gained steam, slowly but surely, for a few years, until 2005, when the United Nations Environmental Program (UNEP) commissioned a study from Freshfields Bruckhaus Deringer, a London law firm that's been around since the mid-eighteenth century. The question UNEP wanted answered was this: "Is the integration of environmental, social and governance issues into investment policy (including asset allocation, portfolio construction and stock-picking or bond-picking) voluntarily permitted, legally required or hampered by law and regulation; primarily as regards public and private pension funds, secondarily as regards insurance company reserves and mutual funds?"[9]

Unsurprisingly, Freshfields determined that incorporating environmental, social, and governance issues into investment policy was not only permissible but practically mandatory. Ignoring these variables, the firm insisted, was the *real* risk to fiduciary responsibility. "Conventional investment analysis," the firm wrote, "focuses on value, in the sense of financial performance. As we noted above, the links between ESG factors and financial performance are increasingly being recognised. On that basis, integrating ESG considerations into an investment analysis so as to more reliably predict financial performance is clearly permissible and is arguably required in all jurisdictions."[10]

The following year, the United Nations launched its Principles for Responsible Investment (PRI), designed to help turn the ideas embraced by the UN and its climate and other environmental standards into practical investment decisions.

Within five years, the governments of New York, California, and Washington were requiring that insurance companies operating in their states disclose climate risk, and CalPERS, the massive $400 billion California Public Employee Retirement System, began looking at climate and water issues as "material" risks.[11] In 2010, the SEC became involved in the issue, discussing disclosure requirements for corporations, given the existing disclosure scheme. Commission Chairman Mary Schapiro stated that "a company must disclose the significant risks that it faces, whether those risks are due to increased competition or severe weather. These principles of materiality form the bedrock of our disclosure framework. Today's guidance will help to ensure that our disclosure rules are consistently applied, regardless of the political sensitivity of the issue at hand, so that investors get reliable information."[12] By the middle of 2017, the ESG movement had become mainstream, as some "1,600 asset owners representing $62 trillion" signed the United Nations PRI.[13]

The old and quaint notion of socially responsible investing, a generally conservative and morality-based position, had morphed into ESG, a much different and much more aggressive proposition altogether.

CHAPTER 7

SETTING THE FIELD

S ection One of this book provides, in detail, the long, complicated historical, ideological, intellectual, and financial conditions leading to the present moment. The road is long but has been trod relentlessly. For more than a century, the responsibility of managing the republic has shifted, remorselessly, from "the people" to the "the powerful." The political Left would have us believe that "the powerful" are those with wealth and money, who advocate greed and selfishness and especially individual autonomy, which gives them the latitude to do as they please. The truth, of course, is almost precisely the opposite. In contemporary America the powerful may, indeed, be wealthy, but they are just as likely not to be. They may very well be men and women of letters and of "proper" experience, a credentialed ruling class, the members of which believe that they are superior to the *hoi polloi*. The advent of public administration and its politics/administration dichotomy gave rise to the notion that people are less fit to govern their own affairs than are the "experts." The creation of the Federal Reserve—not just its creation, but the manner and purpose of its creation—confirmed this notion, guaranteeing that the "experts" in finance would always be those who were the closest to power and the most eager for more.

Likewise, the psychoanalytic philosophers guided their credo of perpetual grievance as it wound its way through the institutions of the West to arrive, in due time, at the center of the educational universe, half-baked and half-understood ideology in hand. They, and those who wished to emulate them but lacked their intellectual capabilities, emasculated the educational system. They ensured that everyone and everything that came after them would be crippled by a lack of intellectual rigor, a lack of decency, and most especially, a lack of knowledge about such erstwhile remedial concepts as right and wrong, truth and lies, good and evil. The pragmatic business consultants turned strategic planning into a moral case for arrogating the invested wealth of shareholders to attend to non-business and heretofore immaterial needs. And the mythmakers of business-academia carefully constructed the legend of the paradoxically avaricious capitalist, who relentlessly pursues his personal advantage, growing ever richer, pushing for boundless short-term treasure, while nevertheless preserving his investments' long-term prospects.

Finally, the noble and godly admonition not to make "any trade which is against the law of God or the law of the land" was taken, shaken, and stood on its head to create an environment in which God and the law of the land have almost nothing to do with the moral judgments offered by those who would choose for the rest of us what trades may be made. The idea that one should not invest in companies whose practices would offend his own sensibilities was turned, by dint of the intellectual and ideological forces extant in the land, into the idea that one should *not be allowed* to invest in companies whose practices offend the financial demigods, whose beliefs and ethics are substituted for those of the average investor.

In 1954, Russell Kirk wrote that "All history, and modern history especially, in some sense is the account of the decline of community and the ruin consequent upon that loss."[1] The trends noted above and detailed previously perpetuate and exacerbate that trend remorselessly. Today, you see, values are to be dictated from above and, moreover, they are to be coerced among the masses by those who know the "values" better, understand them more intimately, and thus can express and utilize them more effectively and benevolently.

Onward, then, to the specifics of the battlefield.

What Is a Public Company?

In everyday language, the word "public" generally refers to something that belongs to everyone equally, a common good that is shared by society as a whole. In business, however, the term means something else altogether. "Public" is short for "publicly traded," which means that the ownership of a company—a corporation, by definition—is freely traded on exchanges or over-the-counter markets to the general public. Anyone with the desire and the wherewithal to buy portions of the company, called "shares" of the company, can do so and can "hold" those shares. That person then becomes an "equity owner."

A "private" company, by contrast, is a company whose ownership is privately held by a person, a family, a group of private investors, etc. One cannot simply "buy" shares in a private company because they are controlled by the owners and are allotted for specific purposes under specific conditions as spelled out in the company's incorporation documents.

Generally speaking, most public companies were once private companies that grew large enough or wished to grow larger and so decided to raise capital by meeting various regulatory burdens and then listing and selling shares of stock.

By way of clarification and explanation of the relevance of the public-private company distinction, consider the case of Chick-fil-A, which illustrates the difference clearly and relevantly to this discussion.

Although there is much confusion as to whether or not Chick-fil-A finally capitulated to its critics in late 2019, the company's position in the face of years of criticism has been remarkably constant. Challenged for their religious beliefs and their donations to Christian groups that espouse traditional Christian beliefs about marriage, the Cathy family has been largely unmoved. They choose to ignore the complaints of their detractors and continue doing their work, providing delicious chicken products to millions of customers and good jobs to more than 25,000 employees. The Cathy family can do so in large part because they are the owners of their business. Chick-fil-A is a private company that is, more or less, answerable only to the very small number of people who own it.

If Chick-fil-A were a public company, however, it would be answerable to all of its shareholders, including activist shareholders who would buy the stock for the sole purpose of challenging the company's policies. Given the success of shareholder activists in pressuring companies on social grounds, it is a virtual certainty that Chick-fil-A would not be the company it is today if it were publicly owned. It would likely have halted its donations to organizations like the Salvation Army and would likely be open on Sundays.

What Are Shareholders? What Is a Director?

A shareholder is just what it sounds like, a person who "holds" a "share" or more of a company's equity stock. As noted in Chapter 5 above, technically and legally, a shareholder owns his shares of the company but is not an owner of the company, per se. He does not have dominion over any specific piece of property, regardless of how many shares he owns. Additionally, as Joseph Bower and Lynn Paine have noted, more than half of all Fortune 500 companies are domiciled in the state of Delaware, where state laws officially vest the power to control the company in the board of directors.[2] The shareholders have the right to elect the board members, but the board has the right to make decisions for the company, which it then delegates to the managers.

Every public company must have a board of directors, a small group of individuals that acts as the fiduciary representative of the shareholders. Board composition varies considerably. The number and type of board members and the election process by which they are selected are set in the corporate bylaws. Directors generally include both insiders—which is to say people who are intimately familiar with the day-to-day operations of the company: executives, former executives, managers, etc.—and outside or independent board members, who are respected, independent individuals from outside the company, who are expected to bring to the corporation a perspective that could not be found internally.

All common stock shareholders have certain rights. They have a right to their portion of the company's profitability, either through stock price appreciation or dividends. They have the right to buy new shares preemptively if the corporation issues new shares. And they have a right to vote and to impress their opinions, through those votes, directly on the directors of the company and indirectly, through the directors, on its managers.

How and When Do Shareholders Have Input?

By law, all publicly traded companies must hold a general meeting once a year, which is why they're called "annual general meetings." All shareholders are invited to attend the meeting and take part in the activities, which generally include a presentation from management, followed by a series of votes. Prior to the meeting, the corporation must submit a document to the SEC, known as DEF 14A or a "proxy statement," which contains all of the details about the meeting—e.g., when, where, proposed executive compensation packages, board of directors candidates, and any other corporate business that requires a vote of shareholders. Time is usually set aside for shareholders to ask questions of the company's management team.

What Is a Shareholder Proposal?

A shareholder proposal is a written request or recommendation submitted by a shareholder to corporate management. In order to submit a proposal, a shareholder must own either $2,000 or 1 percent of the company's stock. Once a proposal has been submitted, the SEC rules on the submission and decides whether or not the company must include it on its annual proxy statement. Generally, the SEC requires the company to list and vote on the proposal, but it can provide a "special exemption."

The shareholder proposal is the primary tool of the corporate activist. By submitting proposals to corporations, activists can either hope that the proposal is popular enough to pass, hope that a proxy advisor supports it, or hope that corporate management will be sufficiently embarrassed by or frightened of public discussion surrounding it that they will negotiate. For decades, most shareholder proposals received very little general support. The rise of coordinated activist investors and proxy advisory services has, however, changed the outlook for many proposals. If corporate managers learn, for example, that one or both of the two dominant proxy services is supporting a proposal, they often seek to preempt the vote by negotiating instead.

By law, shareholders who introduce proposals are not allowed to campaign for their proposals, as such campaigning would constitute a solicitation. The advent of large, widely used, and conflicted proxy advisors has, in many cases, rendered this anti-solicitation provision moot. By definition, proxy advisory services are able to coordinate votes in ways that regular shareholders cannot.

What Is a Proxy?

Although some larger shareholders who have the means to do so attend annual meetings in person, many shareholders cannot and therefore do not. Because they are not in attendance, these shareholders do not get to vote at the meeting, although they do still get to vote. They can either vote by mail or assign their vote to a "proxy." A proxy is someone who attends the meeting and votes on behalf of the shareholder. A shareholder using a proxy must have a formal agreement in place with the proxy and may be required to provide him/her with legal power of attorney. Registered investment managers are often the proxy voters for fund shareholders or large institutional and high-net-worth clients.

What Is a Proxy Service or Proxy Advisory Service?

A proxy service or proxy advisory service is a company that provides a variety of products, research, and execution services primarily to large asset managers (institutional investors, mutual funds, hedge funds, ETFs, etc.). These asset managers hold a majority of publicly traded company shares in the United States. They are authorized to vote the shares of the assets they hold on behalf of their clients. As registered professionals, asset managers are also required by various regulations and other legal protections to vote their clients' shares. In so doing, they are also required to vote their clients' interests, rather than their own, and to perform the due diligence necessary to do so knowledgeably. There are costs associated with all of this, particularly the due diligence.

As a result, many asset managers retain the services of a proxy advisory service, which can handle many of the tasks associated with the proxy process for the manager at far less cost. The proxy service handles the due diligence research and makes recommendations to the asset manager about how to vote his/her clients' shares.

While asset managers are constrained by a well-developed and time-tested body of regulations, proxy advisory services are not; they are, in fact, subject to very few regulatory requirements.* Additionally, the data available suggests that proxy advisory services are far less supportive of management than are asset managers and tend not to be as concerned about their recommendations reflecting the interests of the clients, rather than their own.[3]

Finally, two proxy advisory services—Institutional Shareholder Service (ISS) and Glass-Lewis—dominate the proxy advisory space in the United States, controlling an astounding 97 percent of all proxy advisory business.

* In November 2019, the SEC proposed new regulatory rules to address issues in the proxy advisory business. The proposed new rules are as follows:

1. "Before a proxy advisory firm distributes its recommendations for a particular shareholder vote to its clients, it would be required to give a company an opportunity to comment on the recommendations...."
2. "In the proxy voting advice that a proxy advisory firm distributes to its clients, the firm would be required, if the company so requests, to include a hyperlink to a company statement responding to the firm's recommendations."
3. "The proxy voting advice would also be required to include disclosures on conflicts of interest, including between the proxy advisory firm and the company. The firm would also have a strong incentive, under revised antifraud provisions, to include disclosure on its methodology and sources."[4]

The SEC's regulatory comment period ended in March 2020, but no date has been set for a vote on the regulations. The expectation is that the rule will be finalized at some point in 2020 and will be in effect for the 2021 proxy season.[5]

CHAPTER 8

THE PLAYERS, PART ONE: ON THE LEFT

With the battlespace identified and the field ready for action, identifying the combatants becomes the next critical job. This is a massively lopsided war. It is, perhaps, unfair to use this comparison and thus appear to besmirch the American soldiers who freed political prisoners and rescued American medical students or, conversely, to appear to praise the New JEWEL Communists. But the battlespace on this issue shapes up very much like the United States military versus the People's Revolutionary Government of Grenada. The disparity in resources and firepower is staggering. One side has all the money and all the weapons, while the other has only its determination and the forces of righteousness on its side.

When this section was written, the intention was to cover the players in this game in one chapter. It didn't take long, however, to realize that doing so would be difficult, given the number of significant players, particularly on the Left. Moreover, by dividing the players into their respective ideological camps and dividing those camps into separate chapters, one may better visualize the ponderousness of the chasm between those who wish to politicize American business and capital markets and those who wish to return those spheres of American society to a more neutral position. This chapter, the one covering the activists who would drive American business to the left for profit and fun, constitutes nearly a quarter of this book, while the next, covering those actively fighting for a more traditional view of business, is one of the shortest.

Asset Managers

The executive-level effort to politicize capital markets and American business more generally is led by many managers from many companies in many sectors—high tech, entertainment, retail, etc. But the greatest leverage is that wielded by large asset management companies. Tim Cook, the CEO of Apple, cannot, for example, do much to influence the social or governance behavior of Peter Thiel, other than to apply peer pressure. And while that peer pressure can be powerful—as Brendan Eich can attest—it is limited in its application.

Asset managers, especially asset managers who dominate the world of index funds and exchange-traded funds (ETFs), can have a significant impact on all sorts of companies in all sorts of sectors doing all sorts of business. That's the whole point of an index or exchange-traded fund. It gives the holder some fraction of ownership of all the companies in an index, providing him with both diversification and the opportunities and responsibilities associated with owning shares of *everything*.

BlackRock

Without question, the asset manager that matters most in this battle is BlackRock, the CEO of which is Larry Fink, the star of the introduction to this book. BlackRock manages more than $7 trillion, making it by far the largest asset manager in the world. And Fink, as noted, is a crusader, a man on a mission who is bound and determined to use the power that other people's money—your money, perhaps—gives him to impose his beliefs on the capital markets and, by extension, on the nation more generally.

BlackRock is known as one of the "Big Three" passive asset managers in the world—along with Vanguard and State Street. This is a true description, but it's also incomplete. While its nearly $5 trillion in assets under passive management—i.e., index funds, ETFs—makes it the largest passive manager in the world, the firm also has significant assets under active management. Indeed, the roughly $2.5 trillion it has under active management would, in and of itself, make BlackRock the sixth-largest asset manager in the world. BlackRock is, in other words, a monster. It is a monster in the passive management business, a monster in the active management business, and a monster that public companies can hardly ignore.

As part of the Big Three, BlackRock has immense and almost shocking power to effect change at whatever companies it chooses to change. And the firm's CEO is a crusader, a fanatic who intends to use this power to go set the world on fire (as St. Ignatius Loyola may or may not have told his Jesuits). This raises a host of very serious concerns—for investors, for consumers, for companies, and indeed, for American democracy.

For starters, the Big Three (of which BlackRock is biggest) holds, on average, about 22 percent of the typical S&P 500 company.[1] This includes "18% of Apple Inc.'s shares . . . 20% of Citigroup, 18% of Bank of America, 19% of JPMorgan Chase, and 19% of Wells Fargo."[2] This gives them immense leverage. Moreover, the fact that the last three names above just happen to be the first, third, and fourth largest wealth management firms in the United States (with $1.35 trillion, $774 billion, and $604 billion in assets under management, respectively) amplifies their power to dominate shareholder decisions exponentially.

Indexers have always insisted that the combined power they wield is irrelevant. "We aren't necessarily aligned on issues," they say, and we certainly don't "coordinate." Except that now they do. On ESG concerns, BlackRock and State Street (see below) are nearly perfectly aligned and they don't need to coordinate, because their ESG research and proxy advisory services (see Bloomberg and ISS below) do the coordination for them. And Vanguard, the third of the Big Three, is not far behind them.

And here's where things get a little bit sticky. Traditionally, active asset managers who were unhappy with the performance of a company—be it for environmental, social, governance, or any other of countless reasons—simply sold the stock. They said, in essence, we don't think you're running your business in a manner that is conducive to the values we embrace, and we won't be a party to that.[3]

Passive asset managers, by contrast, do not have that option. They own the company because they own every company. And they cannot walk away from any of them. Therefore, passive managers have two choices: They can simply ignore management and governance issues, hoping that the market will eventually sort the matter out; or they can use their power to change the company—its management, its directors, its policies, even its business plan. Historically, passive managers have chosen the former.[4] Increasingly, however, they're choosing the latter, in part because they're so big now that they *are* the market, and in part because they're led by zealots.

Additionally, BlackRock is one of the largest American investors in the People's Republic of China and would like very much to expand its operations there. In his March 29, 2020 letter to shareholders, Fink wrote, "Our focus on long-term opportunity and structural change is also reflected in the way we approach growing markets, such as China. I continue to firmly believe China will be one of the biggest opportunities for BlackRock over the long term...." Note that this letter was sent *after* the COVID-19 pandemic had hit the United States, after the COVID-19 pandemic had caused a massive disruption in the American economy, after BlackRock was named by the Federal Reserve to administer and manage significant portions of the Fed's emergency debt purchase programs, and literally days before the Chinese company Luckin Coffee blew up in BlackRock's face. Nevertheless, Fink continued, "China's $14 trillion asset management industry is the third-largest in the world, and as the Chinese market opens to foreign asset managers, our global reach and whole-portfolio approach will help us become the leading foreign asset manager in China."[5] True to his word, less than forty-eight hours later, Fink and BlackRock applied to the China Securities Regulatory Commission to establish a mutual fund operation in China.[6]

BlackRock is also heavily invested in Chinese companies and various other companies that do business in China, some of which would never pass Larry Fink's religious precepts if they were American companies. At the end of 2019, the single stock that BlackRock held more of than any other was Apple Inc., which (see below) is rather firmly tied to the anchor of the Chinese Communist Party and is one of the most deceptively "green" companies on the planet. At of the end of the first quarter of 2020, BlackRock held more than 7 percent of all outstanding shares of PetroChina listed on the Hong Kong Exchange.[7] PetroChina, of course, is the listed arm of the state-owned China National Petroleum Company. Not only is PetroChina notoriously un-green, but it also has a long history of social and political problems. In 2000, when the company brought its initial public offering (IPO) to the American market in conjunction with its American banker, Goldman Sachs, a broad coalition of interests on both the political Left and the Right boycotted the offering.[8]

Among other things, PetroChina's parent company (China National Petroleum Company) was doing business with and thereby funding the regime of Omar al-Bashir in Sudan, which was then and remains a State Department–sanctioned state sponsor of terrorism. Additionally, al-Bashir's regime was waging a civil war against the black and animist people of South Sudan and permitted the growth of the modern-day slave trade in Khartoum.

As noted in the introduction to this book, BlackRock has, as of January this year, officially aligned itself with the environmental goal of sustainability. "We believe," CEO Fink wrote in a letter to CEOs in January, "that sustainability should be our new standard for investing." Ironically, it is clear that what he meant by that is that it should be the new standard for investing in *American* companies alone. Chinese companies like the ones Fink and BlackRock invest in don't have the same sort of governance and reporting standards that American companies do, which means that they can, more or less, do whatever they want. And as long as their financial statements don't acknowledge any wrongdoing, there's not a damn thing any American can do about it. That, in turn, means that Fink et al. intend, quite literally, to ensure that American companies are at a competitive disadvantage compared to Chinese companies. And they intend to do so in the name of "sustainability."

State Street

State Street is the third-largest passive asset management company in the country. Like BlackRock, it holds significant portions of most of the companies in the American stock exchanges, and also like BlackRock, it has decided that ESG and sustainability issues will guide its interactions with the managers of the companies it holds. On May 20, 2020, at the State Street annual shareholder meeting—which was held virtually because of the COVID-19 pandemic—State Street CEO Ronald O'Hanley reaffirmed that position and reinforced his company's plans to be an aggressive, activist shareholder. Scott Shepard, who is the coordinator of the Free Enterprise Project, a project of the National Center for Public Policy Analysis (see below), asked O'Hanley about these subjects. "Especially during the economic crisis that is following on the heels of the pandemic lockdown," Shepard began, "how can you justify using your clients' shareholder status to apply a legally suspect concentration of market power to demand changes that do not serve their or national economic interests?"[9]

O'Hanley responded, in part saying, "Any position or stewardship activity that State Street performs is with that sole goal, of ensuring long-term shareholder value creation. Ultimately it's not our decision what companies do, and ultimately we will remain invested in those companies, but because we do not have the ability to not be invested in them, we take the stewardship role seriously and we will continue to do so."[10]

There is an implicit threat in O'Hanley's statement, a threat to the companies that comprise its ETFs, whose shares it holds. To wit: Just because we engage in passive management, don't think that we are going to be passive shareholders. We will not be. Moreover, we're not going away, because we can't go away. This is the same sentiment expressed several years ago by F. William McNabb III, then the CEO of Vanguard (the third of the Big Three), who said, "We're going to hold your stock if we like you. And if we don't. We're going to hold your stock when everyone else is piling in. And when everyone else is running for the exits. That is precisely why we care so much about good governance."[11]

In 2018, State Street became the "sub-manager" of an $800 million ESG fund offered by Domini Impact Investing, which is considered a pioneer both in ESG investing and in shareholder activism to pursue ESG compliance from corporate management. Amy Domini, the founder and CEO of the eponymous firm, was also the socially responsible investing researcher who, in 1990, launched the Domini 400 Index, the first index of its kind. The ESG fund, which represents only part of Domini's offerings, was woefully underperforming the market at its previous advisor, Wellington Management Company. Over three years, the Domini fund "returned 22.8% compared to the average Multi-Cap Core fund, which was up 31% and the S&P 500 index's 42.46%."[12] Amy Domini decided, apparently, that that was a function of management rather than an overall investment strategy.

Others

Domini Impact Investing prides itself on its ESG offerings and on its activist approach to shareholding. The firm, which manages just over

$2 billion in assets, submitted eleven shareholder proposals in 2017.[13] In 2000, Amy Domini was named to *Barron's* "All-Century Team—The 25 Most Influential People of the Century on Mutual Fund Trends."[14]

Walden Asset Management is another Boston-based asset management firm that specializes in ESG investing and corporate shareholder activism. Founded in 1975 as part of the Trust Company of Boston (a New England regional bank), Walden is the oldest socially responsible asset management company at any bank.[15] It manages just under $4 billion in assets and makes its impact both in selective asset holding and in shareholder activism. In 2018, Walden partnered with seventy-four other left-wing activist shareholder groups to file one shareholder petition at fifty different companies, demanding information about company lobbying activities, particularly activities that were in opposition to shareholder activism.[16]

Walden is also the firm most responsible for pressuring the Big Three passive asset management firms to get more involved in shareholder activism. In 2017, Walden offered a shareholder proposal at Vanguard asking the company to change its voting practices to align more with the ESG movement.[17]

There are dozens of other small asset management firms that specialize in ESG and especially shareholder activism. Among the more prominent are Trillium Asset Management, NorthStar Asset Management, and Green Century Capital Management. Most large asset management firms now also offer ESG products (Fidelity, JPMorgan, Goldman Sachs, Bank of New York, etc.).

Bridgewater Associates

In addition to traditional asset management companies, there are also hedge funds that play an important and disconcerting role in the politicization of capital markets. In simple terms, a hedge fund is an investment vehicle that is less regulated than traditional funds and therefore requires that investors—usually legally defined as "limited partners"—be more sophisticated about investment strategies and risks and be "accredited." Traditionally, hedge funds pool clients'/partners' resources and invest in various leveraged strategies, using more risky investment methodologies but usually "hedging" the investment against too much or total risk.

Among the most famous and successful hedge fund managers in the world is Ray Dalio, the founder of Bridgewater Associates.

Dalio, whose net worth is in the $15–$20 billion range, is a devoted and unabashed fan of the People's Republic of China, which he insists is the economy of the future, and a remorseless critic of American capitalism, which he believes is "not working" and is crushing the American dream.

In a famous April 2019 "analysis," Dalio wrote that capitalism is broken, that "it must be reformed to provide many more equal opportunities and to be more productive," that the reformation must come from the "top down," and that it must be concerned with "double bottom line" investing.[18]

Unfortunately, Dalio is long on rhetoric, short on specifics, totally ignorant of causation, and patently hypocritical. His own charitable foundation was established with the donation of a mere 0.5 percent of his net worth, and his insistence on double bottom line investing demonstrates a lack of understanding of the concept. What he favors, actually, is compelling everyone to embrace big-state, top-down ideas that have proven inadequate time and again for at least fifty years. Meanwhile, he insists that "America's position in the new world order will depend on issues such as quality of education, work ethic and the respect for law." And he says all of this with a straight face, even as he gleefully says, the very next moment, that "China will emerge as the dominant power once the dust settles."

Dalio is almost certainly more "invested" in China than any other asset manager in the country, save, perhaps, Larry Fink and BlackRock.

CalPERS

On top of all of this, there are asset management operations that are not private companies, but government operations established to manage public pension money. The biggest and best known of these is CalPERS, the California Public Employees Retirement System. With over $360 billion in assets, CalPERS is the largest public pension fund in the country. It is also one of the most aggressively activist and aggressively "green" public pension funds, despite having some $150 billion in unfunded liabilities.

According to a December 2017 report from the American Council for Capital Formation (ACCF), "One key factor behind this consistently poor performance, according to the ACCF report, is the tendency on the part of CalPERS management to make investment decisions based on political, social and environmental causes rather than factors that boost returns and maximize fund performance."[19] The report also noted "that four of the nine worst performing funds in the CalPERS portfolio as of March 31, 2017, focused on supporting Environment, Social and Governance (ESG) ventures. None of the system's 25 top-performing funds was ESG-focused."[20]

In 2000, during the aforementioned IPO for PetroChina, a group of conservative and liberal activists pushed hard to convince asset managers not to participate. CalPERS was one of the biggest and best-known firms to state publicly that it would not participate.[21] And yet, today, CalPERS has more than $3 billion invested in China, including some investments that have stirred up national security concerns. In March 2020, Trump administration National Security Advisor Robert O'Brien stated that "Some of the CalPERS investment policies are incredibly concerning."[22] That same month, *The Washington Post* reported that "holdings include Chinese military contractors such as China Shipbuilding Industry Corp. and companies currently sanctioned by the Commerce Department for building surveillance and internment camps in Xinjiang, such as Hikvision," and that "Ben Meng, CalPERS's chief investment officer and a U.S. citizen who grew up in China, once was connected to a Chinese Communist Party recruitment effort called the Thousand Talents Program ... [and] admitted his past connection to Thousand Talents" in February 2020.[23]

The New York City Employees' Retirement System (NYCERS) is another large public pension plan that is heavily invested in ESG and suffering subpar returns because of it. In January 2018 Mark Perry, a scholar at the American Enterprise Institute (AEI) and a professor of economics and finance at the University of Michigan's Flint campus, noted that "the 12 worst-performing private equity funds in the New York City Retirement System in 2016 focused on renewable and clean energy assets."[24] A 2019 report from the New York City comptroller showed that the city's unfunded pension and other liabilities were in the neighborhood of $200 billion, larger than those of any other city in the country and most states as well.[25]

Proxy Advisory Services

Two companies—Institutional Shareholder Services (ISS) and Glass Lewis—dominate this space, accounting for 97 percent of the proxy advisory business.

ISS, by far the larger of the two services, is notoriously pro-activist in its proxy recommendations—and this label, "pro-activist," applies in both senses of the term: "activist" investors looking to take control of corporate boards of directors and political "activists" looking to impose their agendas on publicly traded companies and, by extension, on the public. ISS's definition of "good governance" almost always entails recommending in favor of shareholder proposals that hew to a very narrow definition of "good," one that promotes progressive political activism.

The other giant in the field, Glass Lewis, is also consistently "pro-activist" in its recommendations. In fact, the company is one of the most prominent and powerful actors in the ESG movement, generally supporting environmental and "good" governance petitions across the board. Glass Lewis is co-owned by the Ontario Teachers' Pension Plan Board, the largest pension system in Canada (essentially, Canada's CalPERS), and the Alberta Investment Management Corporation, which also runs Canadian government pension money.

In a 2013 policy paper titled "The Troubling Case of Proxy Advisors," the Institute for Governance of Public and Private Organizations, a Canadian good-governance think tank, noted that the most obvious and most troubling aspects of the advisory proxy business include "Lack of transparency as to the process by which they arrive at formulating their recommendations; Inaccuracies in their analysis and unresponsiveness to corporate demands for corrections; [and] Conflicts of interest, in particular for ISS, by their offering of several services to the same corporations which are the subject of their proxy recommendations...."[26]

The conflict of interest for ISS is significant, lucrative, and damning. Traditional institutional research departments, usually run by large brokerage houses, provide research on companies to asset managers and others. They evaluate the company on a variety of measures and then recommend that their clients "buy," "sell," or "hold" these companies' shares. When Thompson/ISS bought the SIRS in 2001, it made a new variety of institutional research available to a much larger audience—one that continues to grow. From that point on, ISS has had the ability to issue buy, sell, or hold recommendations to institutional investors based on the socially responsible nature of the businesses it evaluates. In and of itself, this would not be a significant issue, but as part of ISS's broader business plan and political agenda, it has created an enormous problem—but one that is nevertheless lucrative for the company.

Today, ISS is the fourth largest third-party ESG ratings service provider in the world. That means it develops its own screens and measures; it sells those screens to institutional clients, helping them "discern" what is or is not proper behavior for a company and what is or is not a proper investment strategy for clients. Then it offers itself as a proxy advisor to those same clients, making recommendations on how to vote on shareholder proposals and performing the proxy votes on their behalf. In other words, ISS is shaping the perceptions of what investors' interests should be and which companies they should invest in, before telling those same investors how to vote those interests. This is institutionalized, corporate "begging the question." ISS is essentially fixing the game by creating shareholders who will, almost by definition, vote the way it wants them to on proposals ISS has decided matter. In this way, utilizing the successor operation to the SIRS, ISS can "create" the votes necessary to compel company management to comply with its wishes. This is coercive, conflicted, and most notably, intended to advance ISS's interests rather than those of the investors.

But it gets worse.

ISS also has a division called ISS Corporate Solutions, which acts as a consultant to corporate clients on how to improve such things as governance, environmental record, pay disputes, etc. The proper term for this type of operation is "protection racket." You buy our protection and we'll make sure your windows don't get broken. You buy our corporate solutions, and we'll make sure that the asset managers we tell to buy your company are also aware that they should vote against any ESG proposals against your management. ISS has all bases and all aspects of the business covered.

Unfortunately, as the Institute for Governance of Public and Private Organizations noted, the decisions that ISS pushes are rarely beneficial to anyone except ISS. With "their definition of 'good' governance and the lack of (or very weak) empirical evidence that their kind of governance has any influence on the performance of companies…these proxy consultants have a vested interest in raising the bar of 'good' governance from year to year to justify their continued employment. They thus become *de facto* generators of new governance rules and the arbiters of compliance to their rules. Yet, these new 'rules' are not vetted nor subjected to the review process mandatory for any new rule proposed by the regulators."[27] It's a monumental scam premised on real needs and real concerns that are exploited, mostly by ISS, which is by far the biggest player in the business.

Labor Activists

It's debatable whether labor activists deserve their own section, given that unions' relevance here is as the managers of assets for union members' pensions, health insurance, etc. And, indeed, the segment above about CalPERS and NYCERS involves the management of a great many public-sector unions. Nevertheless, because private-sector unions often have interests that differ from those of public-sector unions, and because they are also a unique force in American politics and society, they get their own brief section.

Public and private unions have different interests and thus also pursue different shareholder activism. Using the terms of stakeholder theory, public and private unions are different kinds of stakeholders. Though both are shareholders whose pensions are tied to corporate returns, they see the process from slightly different perspectives. A significant percentage of public-sector shareholder proposals deal with policy and government lobbying.[28] Public-sector unions don't want companies spending money trying to influence government to spend money or not spend money on specific projects. Private-sector unions don't especially care what corporations do with respect to government, as long as the corporations stay in business and continue to make money and provide jobs and returns.

Additionally, on April 23, 2018, the Department of Labor issued Field Assistance Bulletin 2018-01, which walked back guidance given by the Obama administration on ESG matters, warning labor asset managers that their fiduciary responsibility under the Employee Retirement Income Security Act of 1974 (ERISA) is to manage private union funds with regard to "financial factors." Some ESG matters may be financially material, but most are not.

Outside Activist Groups and Individuals

For most of their history, the American capital markets have been dominated almost exclusively by those with an explicitly business-related purpose for their involvement. Whether they were businesses looking for capital, individuals and firms looking to invest their capital, or institutions dedicated to facilitating the process, the players were nearly all operating under the assumption that they and everyone else were there to build, enhance, and strengthen businesses. That began to change pretty quickly in the late 1980s and early 1990s, however, when it became clear to activists that they, too, could use the capital markets—only in their case, it was to advance political and social agendas that were "too important" to leave to the democratic process.

As You Sow

As You Sow is almost certainly the best known and most active nonprofit activist organization dedicated principally to shareholder activism. As You Sow was founded in 1992 in Oakland, California, to focus on a series of social and environmental activist goals. The organization raises and spends in the neighborhood of $2 million per year; it spends about half on salaries and benefits for employees and half on its campaigns of shareholder activism.[29] In 2019, As You Sow "engaged" with companies on an absolutely staggering ninety-three shareholder proposals, roughly half of which resulted in corporate capitulation and negotiation with the organization.[30]

In its eighty-eight–page 2020 shareholder "Proxy Preview," As You Sow made it clear that it intends to use the otherwise symbolic gestures of organizations like the World Economic Forum and the Business Roundtable as evidence that their agenda has momentum and that the agenda should, therefore, be pushed more aggressively. "[A] new era has dawned!" CEO Andrew Behar triumphantly crowed.[31] Among other things, the "Preview" noted that "Proponents have filed at least 429 shareholder resolutions on environmental, social and sustainable governance issues for the 2020 proxy season, up from 366 filed at this time in 2019," and that "Proponents have already withdrawn slightly more proposals than they had last year at this time—78, compared with 71 in mid-February 2019 and 62 in 2018." And withdrawals, as everyone in the business knows, generally mean negotiation/capitulation.[32]

In noting the subjects of the shareholders' proposals before American corporations, As You Sow probably revealed a bit more than it wanted to. "Corporate political activity makes up the largest single category [of proposal] (18 percent)," the authors wrote, "while those on the environment (mostly on climate change) account for another 21 percent. Roughly even slices of 9 percent to 13 percent come from those about board diversity and oversight, decent work, human rights and sustainability. About 7 percent relate to diversity in the workplace, 5 percent are from conservatives and the remaining 3 percent concern other issues."[33]

The disdain in that last sentence practically drips off the page. Ugh, 5 percent are from conservatives. (Boo!) Not only does this demonstrate the disparity between what the Left is doing versus what the Right is doing—Leftist environmental proposals alone constituted four times the number of conservative proposals—but it also clearly shows that As You Sow (and others) consider themselves political activists, first and foremost. If they thought in terms of business and the true benefit of shareholders, they would also think of proposals differing from theirs in other than political terms. The fact that they see themselves and their allies as distinct from conservatives is an admission of intent to disregard fiduciary responsibility in pursuit of political ends. It really is an amazingly self-unaware but revealing bit of sophistry.

Additionally, As You Sow has made a concerted effort to silence pro-business groups. Under the guise of concern about transparency and accountability, As You Sow pressures corporations to distance themselves from and disavow trade groups and business organizations like the Business Roundtable, the U.S. Chamber of Commerce, and the National Association of Manufacturers. They push the dissociation as an exercise in reputational-risk avoidance, never acknowledging that this, too, is an example of institutionalized corporate "begging the question." The only reputational risk is that which was created by As You Sow, specifically for the purpose of deceiving shareholders into believing that companies face reputational risk from their association with these organizations. It's pure political hardball—with the emphasis on "political."[34]

Two other organizations play significant roles in the politicization of business. Both are fairly well known and are known by their acronyms. One of these is the SPLC—the Southern Poverty Law Center—which bills itself as an organization "dedicated to fighting hate and bigotry and to seeking justice for the most vulnerable members of our society."[35] The second is the HRC—the Human Rights Campaign—which is "the largest national lesbian, gay, bisexual, transgender and queer civil rights organization."[36]

Human Rights Campaign

The former of these two will be discussed at length in a subsequent chapter (on Amazon), and so for now, HRC is the matter at hand. Unlike most of the players in this game, HRC does not spend a great deal of time dealing with or attempting to manipulate the capital markets. Nevertheless, it is still among the most powerful forces politicizing American business. Its power is, in fact, shocking. For an organization with roughly half the number of members of the National Rifle Association (NRA) and a significantly lower profile, HRC nonetheless commands an almost unimaginable amount of attention and deference from America's CEOs.

HRC was founded in 1980, merged with the Gay Rights National Lobby five years later, and was molded into a political force when Elizabeth Birch, the former director of litigation for Apple Inc., took over direction of the organization. Under Birch's leadership, HRC became one of the quietest yet most potent and aggressively political organizations in the country.

HRC's primary tool for wielding influence with business is its "Corporate Equality Index," which rates companies for their acceptance and promotion of lesbian, gay, bisexual, transsexual, and queer (LGBTQ) men and women and the corporate and public policies that affect them directly. The Corporate Equality Index has become an enormous concern for companies that desperately want to avoid the label "homophobic" and thus do everything they can to appease and ally with HRC.

In 2019, HRC had more than $45 million in revenue,[37] the overwhelming majority of which came from corporate and nonprofit donations. HRC's corporate sponsor list is a veritable Who's Who of American business, including: Accenture, Alaska Airlines, Amazon, American Airlines, Ameriprise Financial, Apple, Boston Scientific, BP, Capital One, Cargill, Carnival Cruise Lines, CenturyLink, Chevron, Citibank, Coca-Cola, Cox Cable, Danaher, Dell, Deloitte, Diageo, Ecolab, Ernst & Young, Goldman Sachs, Google, Guardian, Hershey, Hyatt, IBM, Intel, J. Crew, Lexus, Lincoln Financial, Lyft, Macy's, Mastercard Microsoft, Mitchell Gold + Bob Williams, MGM Resorts, Morgan Stanley, Nationwide Insurance, Nike, Nordstrom, Northrop Grumman, Pepsi, Pfizer, PNC, Shell, Symantec, Target, West Elm (Williams Sonoma & Pottery Barn), UBS, UPS, US Bank, and Whirlpool. Household names, one and all.

The strategy that HRC has mastered in pursuit of its goals of changing corporate America is itself a bit of a wonder. HRC changes its criteria for corporate social responsibility constantly. Its Corporate Equality Index will demand one behavior one year, a different behavior the next year, and then a third behavior altogether the year after that. Moreover, the changes in the index follow no coherent pattern. The variables included sometimes appear perfectly arbitrary. Given this, company ratings can and do change from year to year, based solely on random increases or decreases in the "points" allotted or subtracted for each behavior. Because of the shifting nature of the index's measures, companies that were once considered strong supporters of gay rights can wind up on the opposite end of the spectrum, even as their policies remain unchanged or have even improved by the old variables' measures.

This is no mere coincidence. Indeed, it is a time-tested strategy on the political Left for maintaining relevance. In his 1963 classic *Conjectures and Refutations: The Growth of Scientific Knowledge*, Karl Popper noted that Marxism's repeated failures forced its defenders to adopt an old "soothsayer's trick" whereby they "predict things so vaguely that the predictions can hardly fail: that they become irrefutable. . . .In some of its earlier formulations (for example in Marx's analysis of the character of the 'coming social revolution') their predictions were testable, and in fact falsified. Yet instead of accepting the refutations the followers of Marx reinterpreted both the theory and the evidence in order to make them agree."[38]

This old "soothsayer's trick" is employed with crude, blunt force by HRC. It tells companies that corporate policies x, y, and z will produce powerful progress for the LGBTQ community but changes its explanations the next year, saying that policies a, b, and c are the real keys to powerful progress for the LGBTQ community. In so doing, it ensures that "powerful progress" is never achieved, meaning that it is *always* important to keep working and striving toward that goal. That's called "moving the goalpost," and HRC makes itself perpetually relevant, while also making the corporations that "support" the Corporate Equality Index perpetually submissive as well as perpetually "generous."

Sustainability Accounting Standards Board

One final activist group worth noting is the Sustainability Accounting Standards Board (SASB), which wants very much to be the approved arbiter of what does and what does not constitute "sustainable" business practice. SASB is interesting and relevant for a handful of reasons. First, it is an activist organization created and funded by activists that seeks to be granted official government sanction to exercise its activism. Second, it is an operation that serves the interests of large passive asset managers over those of small, active asset managers. And last, it will lead our present conversation away from the activist groups on the Left in the capital markets politicization space and to the activist individuals on the Left.

SASB is a nonprofit organization that was started in 2011 by Jean Rogers. Shortly thereafter, it became, more or less, an operation of Bloomberg LP. Bloomberg Philanthropies made its first grant to the organization in 2012 and continues its heavy support to this day. In an interview on the organization's website, Curtis Ravenel, who was then the director of sustainable business and finance for Bloomberg LP and an SASB foundation board member, stated that "Bloomberg is a founding partner of SASB and now that the standards have been published our work will only continue."[39] Michael Bloomberg, the former mayor of New York, a Democratic presidential hopeful and the founder of Bloomberg LP, served as the chairman of the board of directors of SASB from 2014 to 2018.

SASB spent several years developing its "materiality" standards, which it finalized in 2018. The standards are sometimes conflicting, not especially transparent, vary from industry to industry, often have little to do with sustainability, and almost entirely reflect left-wing priorities that are informed by the neopragmatism of the stakeholder theory movement and the general academic Leftism noted in the previous section of this book. Indeed, the previous section of this book was meant to explain how and why the standards embraced by the organizations and individuals in this chapter have created a self-reinforcing left-wing feedback loop. The academics provide the "moral" justification for the market agitators to do as they wish—and as they would have otherwise, even without the justification. The market agitators leverage their power and financial strength to affect business and capital markets and then use their high-profile positions and their profits to lend practical credibility to the theories of the stakeholder genre and academic Leftism. And round and round it goes.

SASB is perpetually agitating to have the SEC adopt its standards as the Commission has adopted the standards of the Financial Accounting Standards Board (FASB). The FASB was started in 1972 and was granted "substantial authoritative support" by the SEC in 1973.[40] SASB would very much like the SEC to do the same for it. The difference, of course, is that financial accounting standards are objective and nearly universal, whereas sustainability standards are both subjective and politically manufactured.

BlackRock and Larry Fink have already demanded that companies start reporting data in compliance with SASB standards, as have Vanguard and State Street. All of the Big Three continue to push the companies they own—which is nearly all the companies in the known universe—to adopt the standards endorsed by SASB.

In this way, SASB has become a *de facto* regulatory agency—and one with no check on it whatsoever, other than the willingness of the rest of the ESG movement to accept its pronouncements. SASB is, in other words, the embodiment of the Wilson-Waldo ideal for public and private management.

Wilson, recall, advocated the separation of the responsibilities of government into distinct administrative and political spheres, the latter of which would reflect the people's desires, while the former conducted the business of the state, free from the ignorance implicit in those desires. Waldo, in turn, argued that the value-neutral expectation of the administrative function of the state was wrong both empirically and normatively. Not only is the administrative function not possible without the application of values, but it is also unjust to expect administrators not to impress their own values on their work. By this formulation, then, the ideal regulatory agency is one that supersedes the will of the people in order to allow expertly trained administrators to apply their own moral framework to the tasks they undertake.

The American government still being one that is, at least technically, of, by, and for the people, however, those people and their elected representatives still manage to get in the way of the best-laid plans of mice and bureaucrats. Sometimes, for example, the people elect a president who reflects their own rejection of the Paris climate dream world. And as a result, government policy is guided, from the top and from the bottom, to resist the adoption of the hopelessly ideological means and the hopelessly utopian ends of said accord.

In such cases, SASB offers a workaround—that is to say, it offers a quasi-regulatory solution to the problem of a disappointingly intransigent electorate. It offers a way for the likes of BlackRock and State Street and Vanguard and all the rest to skirt the will of the people and have a different regulatory regime imposed from the top down, one that reflects the values of the financial and political elites and cannot be interfered with by the selfish, ill-informed, and inexpert *canaille*.

In his letter to clients in January 2020, Fink wrote, "BlackRock believes that collaboration between investors, companies, regulators, and others is essential to improving the management of sustainability questions." This seems innocuous enough. But then he continues: "We are a founding member of the Task Force on Climate-related Financial Disclosures (TCFD), and a signatory to the UN's Principles for Responsible Investment. BlackRock recently joined Climate Action 100+, and prior to joining, BlackRock was a member of the group's five sponsoring organizations. Climate Action 100+ is a group of investors that engages with companies to improve climate disclosure and align business strategy with the goals of the Paris Agreement."

Note that none of the organizations or agreements identified here have anything whatsoever to do with actual American government "regulators." They are, in fact, extra-regulatory standards created specifically to circumvent the U.S. government and to establish an ideal regulatory machine, answerable only to its members and not to the typically ignorant and intrusive masses. Fink says he and BlackRock believe in "collaboration" with regulators, but it's clear that what he means is that they believe government regulators are too constrained by the democratic and republican forces that manage them to be of much use in advancing the broader cause. Therefore, BlackRock carefully and consciously elides the official regulators, creating their own.

This is the process enabled and encouraged by SASB, and it is also the reason SASB is so important to the ESG crowd. It enables the development of an administrative regime that is independent of the will of the people.

Sadly, as with ISS above, it gets worse—and in much the same manner.

Michael Bloomberg

Although SASB was not Michael Bloomberg's brainchild, it's his baby now. And while Michael Bloomberg is many things—a nanny-stater, a megalomaniac, a ruling-class egotist—first and foremost, he is an incredibly successful capitalist. He's worth $60-plus billion, the bulk of it earned by providing people with the information they need to navigate the capital markets. And he is doing so with ESG and SASB as well. Above, it was noted that "ISS is the fourth largest third-party ESG ratings service provider in the world." Well, the biggest such ratings service is Bloomberg, which "began providing ESG data for companies on the Bloomberg Terminal a decade ago."[41] Additionally, there's Bloomberg Professional Services "with additional solutions for ESG investing," including "the Bloomberg SASB ESG index family," which employ a "methodology [that] was designed around an analytical framework and industry-specific standards developed by the Sustainability Accounting Standards Board (SASB)."[42]

Nice work if you can get it, eh? Create a set of principles that serve as an effective extra-governmental regulatory regime and then turn the monitoring of that regime and investment in those who comply with it into nice multibillion-dollar side gigs. Meanwhile, all you have to do is hope that no one figures out that you created a problem specifically so that you could solve it.

Finally, Michael Bloomberg has an entire mainstream media operation that is able and often willing to amplify the virtues that he signals to a wide and fairly sophisticated audience. Much was made of the announcement, issued during Bloomberg's brief presidential campaign in 2020, that Bloomberg Media (news, opinion, etc.) would not cover the big boss's flaws and would not write critically of him while he campaigned. It didn't matter in that case, of course, since Bloomberg flamed out spectacularly, but it served as a fairly clear indication that, in general, the big boss's whims and preferences play an outsized role in the news and editorial decisions his media empire makes.

In many ways, Bloomberg's billionaire/media kingpin image was an inspiration to many of his fellow billionaires—including some of his friends and cohorts at various climate activist groups. The most obvious such friend was the man who reportedly called Bloomberg and begged him to run for president: the world's richest man, Jeff Bezos. Bezos, of course, founded Amazon.com and bought the *Washington Post* in 2013 for just the loose change he found in his sofa cushions. In February 2020, he pledged $10 billion to be used to address climate change. But again, since Amazon will be discussed in a later chapter, the rest of that story can wait for later.

Laurene Powell Jobs

In the meantime, in 2017, Bloomberg's friend and fellow member of the Climate Leadership Council, Laurene Powell Jobs, bought *The Atlantic*. Technically, her for-profit charitable organization, Emerson Collective, bought the magazine, but because she and the Collective are, more or less, one and the same, that's another distinction without a difference. In addition to owning a majority stake in *The Atlantic*—a magazine that was fairly aggressively pro-China during the COVID-19 pandemic—Powell Jobs also owns a majority stake in *Axios* (a digital-only news source whose editor-in-chief, Nicholas Johnston, was formerly at Bloomberg, LP) and a live-performance news source called *Pop-Up Magazine*.[43]

Powell Jobs is, of course, the widow of Steve Jobs, the late founder of Apple, Inc. When he died in 2011, Jobs left his wife two enormous piles of stock, about $500 million in Apple and a staggering $11.1 billion in Disney, which Mr. Jobs received as part of the deal to sell his digital media company Pixar to Disney. From 2011 through 2016, Powell Jobs was the single largest shareholder of the Walt Disney Company, holding about 8 percent of the company's stock. She cut that stake in half in late 2016,[44] but is still one of the largest individual shareholders of the House of Mouse.

During the period in which Powell Jobs was the largest shareholder of Disney, the company followed her husband's company's lead and bet heavily on and invested heavily in China, the world's largest consumer of coal and the world's largest greenhouse gas emitter. These two companies, like Amazon, have their own chapters later in this book, as great "woke" frauds. For the time being, it should suffice to say that Laurene Powell Jobs—as a philanthropist, as an activist, as a businesswoman, as a political donor, and as a shareholder—has been among the most aggressively "progressive" billionaires in the country, if not the world.

She has used Emerson Collective and other organizations that she's funded to push a variety of progressive causes, especially the case for coercing businesses to curb carbon emissions. She is also a very important, very generous, and very sought-after political donor, who backed Hillary Clinton in 2016 and invested significantly in "get out the vote" and voter registration projects for the 2020 election.[45] She's a significant player in a variety of worlds—business, media, politics, tech—pursuing a hardcore Leftist tack in each.

Marc Benioff

That said, as tech billionaires turned media moguls and woke-scolds go, Powell Jobs is a piker compared to Marc Benioff, the founder, chairman, and CEO of Salesforce and, as of 2018, the owner of *Time* magazine. Benioff is highly regarded by many in business, politics, and the media, largely because he has been very outspoken about social issues and the problems he sees in the American political and economic systems. He has donated to a number of organizations dedicated to achieving largely left-wing political and social ends, and has made an enormous production of having his company boycott states that pass laws that offend his political sensibilities. Having made his billions as a cutthroat capitalist, Benioff is now, more or less, a corporatist.

Benioff is known to be a devotee of Klaus Schwab, the German engineer and economist who founded the World Economic Forum.[46] Schwab famously penned the "Davos Manifesto" of corporate ethics in 1973, and his organization hosts the late-January annual meeting in the town of the same name, where the world's glitterati gather to discuss how best to let the people eat cake. Davos, of course, is the epitome of top-down, paternalistic business and economic management, and Schwab is its leader, a man who believes that the world can be a much better place if the great men and women would all just think a little bit more about the poors as they drink their champagne and nibble their caviar. Davos is to the modern era as Roberto Callasso described the Congress of Vienna, the "infected gauze that would bandage the world."[47]

As a Schwab enthusiast, Benioff has made it his business to ensure that anyone who has anything to do with his company—all the stake-holders, you might say—contribute equally to his favored political and social causes. "At my company, Salesforce," Benioff wrote, "we baked philanthropy into our business model from day one, leveraging one percent of our technology, people, and resources to help nonprofits around the world achieve their missions." In practice, what this means is that Benioff has given away "more than $100 million in grants...more than 1.1 million [employee] volunteer hours and...products to more than 27,000 organizations."[48] Just to be clear, as of the moment this book is being written, Benioff is worth more than $7 billion, which means that $100 million would be about 1.4 percent of his personal wealth. But he's had his "shareholders" give that money away instead. Just because he can.

Benioff also believes—as does Schwab—that the world needs a "new" form of capitalism. "Over the past 20 years, the company that I co-founded, Salesforce, has generated billions in profits and made me a very wealthy person," Benioff wrote in the *New York Times*. "Yet, as a capitalist, I believe it's time to say out loud what we all know to be true: Capitalism, as we know it, is dead." He continues, noting that "capitalism as it has been practiced in recent decades—with its obsession on maximizing prof-its for shareholders—has also led to horrifying inequality," and that "[w]hen government is unable or unwilling to act, business should not wait."[49]

Here again, it's fairly clear that the Left's conception of the new and improved politics-administration dichotomy is what motivates Benioff to act: the people are too dumb to understand the problem and therefore need to be told what to do by "experts" who not only know more than the average person but also have "better" values. The irony is that the capitalism Benioff excoriates here is not exactly capitalism as

Adam Smith or even Milton Friedman would recognize it. It is, rather, the grossly distorted ladder that Benioff and his ilk used to climb to the heights of financial power and privilege, but now wish to pull up behind themselves—mostly, one would hope, out of embarrassment at their own behavior.

It's hardly surprising that Benioff would want to change capitalism and to do it on the backs of his shareholders. That is, essentially, how he has done everything in his life since he launched Salesforce in 1999. The market commentator (and erstwhile political science professor) Ben Hunt has called Benioff "one of the modern-day robber barons," noting that Benioff and those like him "built multi-billion dollar personal fortunes out of serial acquisitions of profitless software companies and constant stock sales. And by constant I mean constant. From 2004 through 2010, under a series of 10b5-1 plans filed with the SEC, Marc Benioff sold at least 10,000 shares of Salesforce.com stock....Every. Single. Day."[50] Hunt has also noted that the "capitalism" that Benioff practices and refers to as "shareholder capitalism" more generally is a specific variety of shareholder capitalism, one that enriches insider shareholders at the expense of common shareholders. "No company has played the stock-based compensation game better than Benioff's brainchild, Salesforce.com," Hunt wrote, "to the benefit of not only Benioff, but everyone in management (particularly sales) at Salesforce. Here's how it works. Since Salesforce became a public company, its revenues have grown at a wonderful clip. Its EBITDA (earnings before interest, taxes, depreciation and amortization) and net income available to common shareholders...not so much."[51] Hunt continued:

> Since it became a public company in 2004, Salesforce.com has paid its employees $4.8 billion in stock-based compensation. That's above and beyond actual cash compensation. For tax purposes, it's actually expensed quite a bit more than that, namely $5.2 billion. The total amount of net income available for common shareholders? $360 million. On total revenue of $52 billion.
>
> Note that none of this includes the money that Benioff himself made in stock sales from 2004 through 2010....[52]

Meanwhile, Benioff has the gall to use his company's inflated profit numbers (which are reported before its executives' stock-based compensation is deducted) to insist that business can be different, that it can be profitable as well as charitable. All that everyone needs to do is follow his top-down Davos-created stakeholder model. "Salesforce is living proof that new capitalism can thrive and everyone can benefit. We don't have to choose between doing well and doing good." It might be more accurate to say that Benioff is doing neither, that he is manipulating the existing financial infrastructure to enrich himself and his colleagues and to alleviate his guilty conscience, all at the expense of his shareholders. Or, again, as Ben Hunt put it, Benioff's schtick "is a *confidence game* in the true sense of the term."

And speaking of confidence games, one last individual playing an enormous but largely unnoticed role in politicizing capital markets and corporate America is Eric Holder, the former attorney general of the United States.

Eric Holder

By all rights, after his work as the Clinton administration's deputy attorney general in 2000, Eric Holder should never have worked in government again—or been trusted by anyone who believes in fairness, justice, or equality, especially anyone connected to the financial markets. Holder, you see, not only facilitated the pardon of fugitive commodities trader Marc Rich, but he also did so surreptitiously, with the probable intent of furthering his own career. Most observers believe that Rich "bought" his pardon, and certainly he did, in a broad sense. In a much narrower sense, however, he didn't need cash to get his pardon so much as he needed an ambitious and unscrupulous man on the inside. That man was Eric Holder. A post-pardon investigation by the House Committee on Oversight and Reform concluded that Holder likely believed that helping Rich get his pardon would benefit his career and, as a result, "Holder failed to inform the prosecutors under him that the Rich pardon was under consideration, despite the fact that he was aware of the pardon effort for almost two months before it was granted."[53] The Committee also concluded that Holder convinced Clinton to use his most important powers to grant unwarranted pardons "to wealthy fugitives whose money had already enabled them to permanently escape

American justice" and that "[f]ew other abuses could so thoroughly undermine public trust in government."[54]

Nevertheless, Barack Obama named Holder to be his attorney general and thus allowed him to escape any consequences for his misdeeds. Indeed, Obama provided Holder with precisely the reward he sought for undermining the rule of law.

Unfortunately, once he was named attorney general by Barack Obama, Holder proceeded to prove all the old theories about the escalation of deviant behavior correct: If a subject gets away with it once, he'll try to get away with it twice, and then thrice, and so on; likewise, if he gets away with small matters, he raises the stakes successively, moving from small matters to large matters and then on to even larger matters. And thus did Eric Holder conduct his legal oversight of the financial services industry in the wake of what was, at the time, the greatest financial collapse since the Great Depression.

By most measures, one would likely conclude that, as attorney general, Holder went very easy on the large Wall Street firms that precipitated the great financial collapse. His Justice Department won zero convictions in court, and they actually tried only a few small-time cases. Instead, Holder decided that it could, theoretically, be too damaging to the economic system to pursue any of the big banks, and so he dealt with them very cautiously and very gently. In so doing, he expanded the problems associated with the financialization of the economy by financializing justice and the rule of law as well. If a company was too big to fail, then its executives, directors, and employees were "too big to jail" as well. In a column penned after Holder had announced that he was leaving DoJ to return to his private legal practice at Covington and Burling, *Rolling Stone*'s Matt Taibbi explained Holder's exceptional value to the Wall Street big boys: "Here's a man who just spent six years handing out soft-touch settlements to practically every Too Big to Fail bank in the world. Now he returns to a firm that represents many of those same companies: Morgan Stanley, Wells Fargo, Chase, Bank of America and Citigroup, to name a few...his service was certainly worth many billions of dollars to Wall Street."[55]

Despite his record of negligence bordering on recklessness—or perhaps because of it—Holder has managed to reinvent himself as a corporate governance guru. In 2017, Uber asked Holder—plus Arianna

Huffington, who is an Uber board member; Uber's HR chief, Liane Hornsey; and Uber's in-house counsel, Angela Padilla—to investigate charges from a female former employee that sexual harassment and sexism were rampant at the company.

Some of what Holder et al. recommended were standard, pro forma good-governance ideas: appoint an independent chairman of the board of directors, fill vacancies on the board with more independent directors, etc. Much of the rest of what they recommended was the usual management-consultant jargon—e.g., "An 'owner' of Human Resources–related policies should be identified or hired...."

After that, however, the committee wandered off into the weeds of progressive good governance ideas, recommending bias training for HR staff, "increasing the profile of Uber's head of diversity and the efforts of his organization," establishing "an employee diversity board," publishing "diversity statistics," and, of course, utilizing a version of the NFL's "the Rooney Rule for women and other underrepresented populations for key positions, wherein each pool of candidates interviewed for each identified position includes at least one woman and one member of an underrepresented minority group, thereby ensuring that members of the populations currently underrepresented in Uber's workplace are interviewed with appropriate consistency."[56]

Again, most of this is pro forma. Holder probably could have saved Uber a pretty penny by just recycling an old report. At the same time, however, the fact that this is pro forma explains a bit about why it's become something of a problem. Many companies lack diversity in various aspects of their operating structure, from employees to managers to executives to directors. And many of these companies could benefit from a more diverse workforce or board. There is no question that employing people from diverse backgrounds, diverse experiences, diverse educational environments, etc. can be beneficial to a company. Varying histories and personal narratives contribute to varying thought patterns and problem-solving strategies. That much is largely inarguable. Nevertheless, one of the most important aspects of such beneficial diversity is *viewpoint* diversity, which is to say diversity in approaches to life, to government, to politics, to business, and so on. Diversity in itself is a noble social goal, but diversity without viewpoint diversity tends to take many of the strictly business-related benefits of the diversity strategy off the table. And in his report, Holder defined diversity specifically as "focusing on the presence of diverse employees based on religion, race, age, sexual orientation, gender, and culture."[57]

Holder's definition of diversity—coupled, of course, with his name recognition and standing—is critically important for three reasons.

First, it created an interpretive framework for the concept of diversity that is not necessarily supported by the law. To be clear: Holder's definition is not wrong or illegal in any sense. But it is in contravention of the spirit of the law as it has been applied. The law in question—the Securities Exchange Act of 1934, as amended in 2009—requires listed companies to disclose and describe their diversity policies for the nomination of directors in their annual proxy statements. In its final rule on the implementation of the diversity question, the SEC specifically and intentionally did not define what diversity should mean, believing that such decisions were best left up to the listed companies.[58] The SEC wrote that it had voted to:

> require disclosure of whether, and if so how, a nominating committee considers diversity in identifying nominees for director....We recognize that companies may define diversity in various ways, reflecting different perspectives. For instance, some companies may conceptualize diversity expansively to include differences of viewpoint, professional experience, education, skill and other individual qualities and attributes that contribute to board heterogeneity, while others may focus on diversity concepts such as race, gender and national origin. We believe that for purposes of this disclosure requirement, companies should be allowed to define diversity in ways that they consider appropriate.[59]

Holder's interpretation overrides this purposefully written regulation, urging shareholders and managers to ignore the SEC's explicit goal and to create a one-size-fits-all approach to diversity.

Second, Holder's definition of diversity was also contradicted by the recommendations for "Common Sense Governance Principles" that were authored and supported by some of the biggest names in American business in 2016. Among the "authors" of these principles were some of the biggest and most powerful players in the capital markets, including four who have already been mentioned in this book: Jamie Dimon of JP MorganChase, Larry Fink of BlackRock,

Bill McNabb of Vanguard, and Ronald O'Hanley of State Street.[60] Toss in the Oracle of Omaha himself, Warren Buffett, and the list of the authors of these common-sense principles reads like a Who's Who of finance. And they defined "diversity" as follows: "Directors should have complementary and diverse skill sets, backgrounds and experiences. Diversity along multiple dimensions, including diversity of thought, is critical to a high-functioning board. Director candidates should be drawn from a rigorously diverse pool....While no one size fits all—boards need to be large enough to allow for a variety of perspectives."[61]

It's clear that before Eric Holder took on the job of defining diversity for Uber, both the government and the leaders of the financial services world believed that diversity should be defined to include "viewpoint diversity." Any value to be gained by engaging a diverse group of directors would be enhanced significantly if the definition of diversity was enhanced to include variables covering diverse social, political, partisan, and intellectual perspectives.

But that is precisely what Holder undermined.

The third reason that Holder's input matters so much is a tautology: it matters so much because it matters so much. Because Holder has anointed himself an expert on diversity, and because the good and decent men and women of corporate America have taken him at his word about his "expertise," his definition of diversity has supplanted the non-definition provided by the SEC and the Common Sense definition carefully crafted by the leaders of the financial services world. The year before he signed on to rework Uber's diversity plans, Holder had been hired by Airbnb to help it revamp its antidiscrimination policies. Three years after that, he was hired by the American Institute of Architects to help them fight racism and systemic bias in their awards presentations. Also in 2019, Holder gave the keynote address at the National Diversity Council's "top 50 general counsel dinner." In short, for a variety of reasons that boggle the mind, Eric Holder has become *the* go-to guy on corporate diversity. And his diversity model explicitly ignores the idea of viewpoint diversity.

In his 2019 letter to CEOs, Larry Fink—co-author of the aforementioned "Common Sense" principles of corporate governance—declared that he was "Unnerved by fundamental economic changes and the failure of government to provide lasting solutions," and insisted that board diversity was one of the keys to corporate leaders fixing what government couldn't or wouldn't.[62] In private comments made around the same time, Fink "told the firm's 14,000 employees that he is instituting potentially the most aggressive diversity program in corporate America, ensuring that 'a bunch of white men' will no longer be running the world's largest money management firm."[63]

To reiterate, diversity is a perfectly sound and reasonable strategy for achieving various shareholder and stakeholder goals. Nevertheless, Fink's purposes here appear somewhat less sound and reasonable, again taking on the Wilsonian role of arbiter of right and wrong in the absence of democratic action and clearly drifting away from the "Common Sense" principles that advocated a broader and more substantive conception of diversity. As "one BlackRock executive who spoke on the condition of anonymity about Fink's remarks" put it, "This isn't about diversity. It's about identity politics and virtue signaling that a CEO of a public company shouldn't be engaged in."[64]

This is the direction in which Eric Holder is pushing both corporate America and its hall monitors, the asset managers who believe that "Society is increasingly looking to companies, both public and private, to address pressing social and economic issues."[65]

A final and important part of this puzzle is the question of whether or not the Holder model "works" in a fiduciary sense. Proponents claim that there are mountains of evidence demonstrating that a Holderesque, narrow, sex- and race-based interpretation of diversity is valuable as a business tool, in and of itself. But the evidence suggests that this is more wishful thinking than fact. For example, in a *Forbes* article in March 2020, a researcher named Bhakti Mirchandani made her case for gender diversity under following headline: "The Results Are In: Board Gender Diversity Is As Important As Revenue Growth In Long-Term Value Creation." The headline has, however, since been changed to reflect a more nuanced approach to the results of the study.[66] But while *Forbes* changed the headline, it did NOT change the lead paragraph, which made a bold statement about gender diversity: "As part of the effort to research long-term value creation across the investment value chain, FCLTGlobal has reached a significant and surprising finding: board gender diversity is as important as revenue growth in predicting a company's long-term success." This was a mistake. *Forbes* should have changed that lede as well as the headline, since it was not supported by the research.

The study in question—"Predicting Long-Term Success for Corporations and Investors Worldwide"—simply did not support the claims made in either the original headline or the lead paragraph. The data collected were incomplete and thus not all that helpful. They indicated a small correlation between board diversity and long-term ROI, but only on a small, unspecified portion of a small percentage of the return on investment. Lastly, it did not indicate *any* causation whatsoever. And this is typical of the literature on the business impact of the narrow, Holderesque interpretation of diversity.[67]

Institutions

All of the organizations in the final section of this chapter are significant players that one might normally expect to be neutral. One is a government agency, after all, while another is a quasi-government entity and the third a multifaceted operation that serves as a semi-official licensing agency, a professional development organization, and a continuing-education provider. All three would seem, in short, to have specific purposes that would dictate at least the pretense of objectivity. And yet all three fail that test and are actively and purposely acting to politicize American business, American finance, and the capital markets.

The Securities and Exchange Commission (SEC)

The Securities Act of 1933 and the Securities Exchange Act of 1934 were the two primary New Deal–era laws passed to federalize and standardize the sale and trading of securities. After the Great Crash of 1929 and amid the Great Depression, the Roosevelt administration believed that the existing state-level "blue sky" securities laws were outdated and thus easy to manipulate and to corrupt. And so, in response, they pushed a number of securities reforms and, upon their passage, placed one of the luckier—and more corrupt—securities magnates in the country in charge of the new independent agency. That man, Joseph P. Kennedy, had made a fortune in the 1920s, trading on inside information, manipulating stock prices, and then, fortuitously, selling all his long positions and shorting the market, just before the Great Crash. Kennedy may or may not have been a bootlegger, but in either case, he was hardly an honest man. And just before taking the SEC job, and just before the end of Prohibition, Kennedy, with the help of Roosevelt's son Jimmy and Winston Churchill, secured the distribution rights to a variety of British spirits, including Dewar's Scotch and Gordon's gin.[68]

Fortunately for everyone, Kennedy did not stay long in the position, and the Commission, under the guidance of men like future Supreme Court Justice William O. Douglas, found its footing and became a trusted, if sometimes overweening, institution.

The role of the SEC in today's capital markets could, of course, be the subject of an entire book—or several. Its role in the politicization of the markets, however, is very narrow but very important and growing more so all the time.

In simple terms, what the SEC is doing is allowing the bias of career staffers to affect the shareholder proposal process in favor of left-leaning shareholders and at the expense of those on the Right. As a general rule, the politically appointed SEC commissioners have been very protective of shareholder prerogatives and rights. As noted earlier in this chapter, the current SEC commissioners are in the process of writing a final rule to help bring a little standardization and transparency to the proxy advisory business, which will, presumably, be a victory for shareholders. As noted earlier in this book, however, *career* public officials are often taught, trained, and encouraged to apply their own values to the execution of their duties and to view themselves as "experts" who are better able to administer public policies than is the public at large, including shareholders. This has created something of a rupture in the SEC's operations, whereby even commissioners appointed by free-market-oriented presidents are unable to pursue the "will of the people" without the undue influence of career bureaucrats, who apply their own personal and entrenched institutional will to new matters as well as day-to-day operations. This is a typical problem with entrenched bureaucracies, of course. But only lately does it seem to have become a more serious issue.

Here's how this works: As a rule—an actual, real, bona fide rule, Rule 14a-8 of the Code of Federal Regulation, pursuant to the Securities Exchange Act of 1934[69]—shareholders have the right to submit proposals and to have those proposals voted on by the rest of the shareholders. The rule also states that "Under a *few specific* circumstances, the company is permitted to exclude [shareholder] proposal[s], but only after submitting its reasons to the Commission."[70] Finally, the rule spells out thirteen specific conditions under which the proposal may be withheld. If a corporation feels that a proposal was unnecessary and could, therefore, be withheld, it petitions the SEC on the matter. The SEC then solicits feedback on the matter from both sides, renders a decision, and notifies both parties. These decisions are usually made by career staff, and if one of the parties disagrees with the decision, it may then request that the commissioners also render a judgment. This appeals process is almost always reserved for especially pressing or widely germane matters.

Starting in the late 1990s, the SEC has amended the rule on several occasions, including a 1998 amendment of the "ordinary-business exception," which allowed a company to have a proposal withdrawn "If the proposal deals with a matter relating to the company's ordinary business operations."[71] In a 2002 Staff Bulletin, the SEC explained the 1998 amendment as follows: "Proposals that relate to ordinary business matters but that focus on 'sufficiently significant social policy issues'... would not be considered to be excludable because the proposals would transcend the day-to-day business matters."[72]

Needless to say, that "sufficiently significant social policies" clause was a ticking time bomb. In 2018, the SEC detonated that time bomb with another memo, one in which the Commission stated, explicitly and unapologetically, that it would use the clause to interpret proposals subjectively,[73] thereby giving staff immeasurable leeway.

Unsurprisingly, in just the short time since SEC staffers granted themselves this leeway, they appear to have begun using it to enforce the activist, interventionist stakeholder model of corporate governance.

During the 2019 shareholder meeting season, Walden Asset Management (see above) submitted a shareholder proposal to CorVel Corporation, in which it resolved that CorVel should issue a report on any risks that might be associated with the omission of sexual orientation and gender identity from its equal employment opportunity policy.[74] SEC staff agreed with Walden that the matter "transcends ordinary business matters,"[75] thereby denying CorVel's request to keep the proposal off its proxy statement.

Not long after, Justin Danhof, chief counsel at the National Center for Public Policy Research's Free Enterprise Project (see Chapter 9), filed a similar shareholder proposal with Apple. The only difference was that Danhof's proposal concerned viewpoint diversity, rather than strict Holderian sexual preference diversity. Indeed, Danhof intentionally reverse-engineered the Walden proposal, using the same language but substituting "viewpoint" and "ideology" for "sexual orientation" and "gender diversity." In this case, the SEC sided with Apple, agreeing that the proposal did, in fact, pertain to ordinary business matters. As Danhof noted, "The only distinction between the two proposals is the party meant to be protected from discrimination, which should in no way change whether the proposals are or are not within the ambit of the companies' ordinary business."[76] Yet his proposal was denied by the SEC staff, even in spite of Apple's failure to respond to the proposal in the time period mandated by SEC rules.[77]

Obviously, one incident is proof of nothing in and of itself. In this case, however, it does suggest that the SEC staff has created conditions under which the appearance of favoritism is likely in the future, even if the actual practice of favoritism is strictly avoided.

The CFA Institute

As noted in previous chapters, American business schools were among the last institutions to fall to the overt politicization of higher education. Nevertheless, the process, once set in motion, produced the inevitable result, and now it is undoubtedly the case that academic instruction in business administration differs relatively little from instruction in public administration, at least where "values," "norms," and "stakeholders" are concerned.

It would be a mistake to say that the CFA Institute is dedicated to ensuring that no one slips through the cracks of indoctrination and winds up supporting free and fair capital markets. There is no grand conspiracy here, no coordination between business schools and the Institute to guarantee that new investment professionals are properly supportive of neopragmatic normative stakeholder models. It would be absurd even to suggest such a scheme.

At the same time, however, it's clear that the CFA Institute is dedicated to ensuring that no one slips through the cracks of indoctrination and winds up supporting free and fair capital markets. It's just that it came to that position on its own, which is not all that surprising. After all, the Institute's board of governors includes the director of Fannie Mae; the global head of active equity product strategy at BlackRock; the co-founder of the Climate Governance Initiative; and a distinguished professor of business administration and dean emeritus at the UVA Darden School of Business, where he's worked alongside stakeholder theory guru Edward Freeman since 1986.[78] Moreover, the Institute is headquartered in Charlottesville, Virginia, and is "affiliated" with 236 university business schools in the United States alone.[79]

The initials CFA stand for Chartered Financial Analyst, which is a designation awarded since 1963, when the Financial Analysts Federation created the Institute of Chartered Financial Analysts to develop a curriculum, to develop a code of conduct, and to administer the charter exam, which is estimated to require one thousand hours of study to pass. Today, the CFA designation is the "gold standard" in professional asset management. The Institute claims, largely without dispute, that its charter holders "represent the best in the investment management industry—employees who are highly skilled and who are bound by the highest ethical standards."[80]

Over the last several years, ESG considerations have come to play a much larger role in the CFA study and exam materials. According to the Institute, it believes that "more thorough consideration of ESG factors by financial professionals can improve the fundamental analysis they undertake and ultimately the investment choices they make."[81] To that end, the Institute is "exploring the development of an ESG investment product standard that would build a framework for investment managers to better communicate, and their clients to better understand, the nature and characteristics of ESG-centric funds and investment strategies."[82]

To facilitate this process, the CFA Institute created a fifteen-person working group on ESG matters. That working group is chaired by Alexis Rosenblum, the chief corporate sustainability officer at BlackRock.[83]

The Federal Reserve/Central Banks

As noted in a previous chapter of this book, the Federal Reserve System was created specifically of the big banks, by the big banks, and for the big banks. And that's mostly how it's behaved for the last century-plus. That's not to say that the Fed has not or does not consider the effects of its policies on the rest of the country and the rest of the world. It does, constantly. It's just that those considerations don't matter as much as the interests of the big banks and big investment firms on Wall Street. That's just the way it works—and the way it was *designed* to work. This is the key to understanding everything the Fed does. It is quasi-governmental, and the president appoints the chairman and the board of governors, yet it answers only to its constituents, the big banks. Everything else is window dressing.

In its pursuit of overtly social and political ends that are far removed from its mission and mandate, the Fed has been aided, pushed, pulled, and prodded by other institutions—the U.S. Senate, the Democratic Party, etc. The most relevant and most powerful accomplices, however, are the Fed's global counterparts—the Bank of England, the Bank of Japan, and the European Central Bank. All have played their part in encouraging the Fed to expand the scope of its efforts to impose on markets an unaccountable, top-down financial infrastructure that explicitly and enthusiastically rewards social and political behavior that serves elite interests and punishes dissent.

The narrative about the "need" for central bank action on climate change in particular first began to take shape in late 2015 and early 2016. On September 22, 2016, Mark Carney, governor of the Bank of England and chair of the Monetary Policy Committee, gave a speech in Berlin in which he worded the narrative very carefully and very provocatively, in language specifically chosen to reframe the case for central bank intervention in financial and fiduciary terms. "A wholesale reassessment of prospects, as climate-related risks are re-evaluated," he warned, "could destabilise markets, spark a pro-cyclical crystallisation of losses and lead to a persistent tightening of financial conditions: a climate Minsky moment."[84] A "Minsky moment" is a market term named for the economist Hyman Minsky, and it is used to designate the point at which a bull market has become so speculative and over-leveraged that it hits a peak and then tips over and crashes. What Carney was saying, in other words, is that he believes a time will come when markets will have better knowledge of the risks associated with climate change, and they will realize, as those risks are processed, that they had speculated wildly on securities that are unsuited for the new climate reality. And then the markets will crash.

This, then, was a watershed in global finance, the moment that the big banks, the monster investment firms, and the world's central banks began framing climate change as a risk management issue rather than good corporate social policy. By insisting that climate change is a fiduciary issue and that anyone who disagrees is betraying his clients' trust, the giants of global finance were not only able to change the narrative but were able to do so by claiming the fiduciary moral high ground as well. Suddenly a whole new realm of risk—and reward—opened up before the central banks and their clients.

Over the following three years or so, some central banks became very interested in involving themselves in the climate change "risk management" business, while others did so reluctantly, only getting involved themselves when they felt compelled to do so. The Federal Reserve, for its part, was cautious. As befits an American enterprise, the Fed took a "wait and see" approach, hoping to *wait* until the BoE and the ECB became more heavily involved to *see* how that worked out.

In March of 2019, however, the Fed decided that it could no longer remain on the sidelines and chose to get into the game. In a March 25 "Economic Letter," Glenn Rudebusch, an executive vice president and senior policy adviser at the Federal Reserve Bank of San Francisco, made the case for the Fed to incorporate climate change concerns and measures into its economic forecasts and policies. "It is essential for Federal Reserve policymakers to understand how the economy operates and evolves over time," Rudebusch wrote. "In this century, three key forces are transforming the economy: a demographic shift toward an older population, rapid advances in technology, and climate change."[85] Ominously, near the end of his letter, Rudebusch concluded that the Fed's policy options are limited, at least for the time being: "Some have advocated that central banks use their balance sheet to support the transition to a low-carbon economy, for example, by buying low-carbon corporate bonds. Such 'green' quantitative easing is an option for some central banks but not for the Fed, which by law can only purchase government or government agency debt."[86]

In a note to clients dated January 24, 2020, the market commentator Rusty Guinn explained why this report was, in his words, such a "Big Deal." "It is important, especially for those who may not deal with these questions every day, to know what is being suggested here. Some economists were—and are—proposing that an unelected body sit in the position of determining by fiat the price at which (and whether!) different companies would be able to access capital based on that body's assessment of whether that institution was deemed to be sufficiently green."[87]

As Guinn noted, the financial press and other "missionaries" spent several months after the publication of Rudebusch's letter preparing the battlespace and mainstreaming the "idea that *subjective* regulatory policy, rather than traditional macroprudential activities, ought to be shifted to an unelected body."[88] By September 2019, the European central bankers were mostly in agreement that they should address climate change, and that they should address it as an existential crisis, as a systemic risk that must underscore every policy they enact. In confirmation hearings before the European Parliament, Christine Lagarde, the former head of the International Monetary Fund, who had been nominated to take over as the director of the ECB, declared her utter fealty to the idea that central bankers should be addressing climate policy. "The primary mandate [of the ECB] is price stability," she told the members of Parliament, "but it has to be embedded that climate change and environmental risk are mission critical."[89]

Four months later, at the 2020 World Economic Forum annual meeting at Davos—the fiftieth such meeting of the global glitterati—the Bank for International Settlements (BIS) released its new book-length report on the subject of climate change and central banking, titled *The Green Swan: Central Banking and Financial Stability in the Age of Climate Change.* In it, the BIS—which is sometimes called "the central banks' central bank"—advanced the narrative even further, supporting the idea that *all* central banks should be prepared to expand their mandates to deal with the threats that climate change could pose to the financial system.

The Green Swan is interesting and relevant for a couple of reasons. First, it is relatively mild and measured, particularly in the context of Davos and the global financial elites' preoccupation with climate change. Its authors are careful to hedge their forecasts and their recommendations. Nevertheless, as Rusty Guinn argued, "even in its hedging, [*The Green Swan*] can't help but restate the emerging arguments for an expanded, open-ended role for central banks."[90]

The second, related reason the book is important is that it does something highly unusual among climate change activists, central bankers, and other financial elites. It explains repeatedly and emphatically that, at present, no one knows anything about climate change for certain. The report makes the following acknowledgments: First, climate models are wildly erratic, wildly varying, and, to date, wildly inaccurate. Second, even if climate models were not erratic and inaccurate, modeling financial best practices based on them would be extremely difficult, complicated, and controversial. Third, traditional risk assessment techniques have no value whatsoever in attempting to model and plan future climate-related financial liabilities, in part because the climate models are wildly inaccurate and in part because we have no precedent by which to measure future risks. And fourth, in spite of all of this, all central bankers—and, by extension, all people whose lives and business activities are affected by central bankers—should use the idea of "climate change" to be prepared for nearly any eventuality.

This is a very nuanced, very careful, very deliberate case, one that warns that human error is a significant risk. Indeed, the BIS acknowledges that central bankers and large financial services firms must be careful in how they approach the problems associated with climate change because if they're not, they could end up making things much worse than they would be otherwise. For example, the authors write: "Transition risks are associated with the uncertain financial impacts that could result from a rapid low-carbon transition, including policy changes, reputational impacts, technological breakthroughs or limitations, and shifts in market preferences and social norms. In particular, a rapid and ambitious transition to lower emissions pathways means that a large fraction of proven reserves of fossil fuel cannot be extracted...becoming 'stranded assets,' with potentially systemic consequences for the financial system....."[91] What this means is that Christine Lagarde and the ECB, Glenn Rudebusch and the San Francisco Fed, and all of the asset managers like Larry Fink and BlackRock would be well advised to proceed with caution so that they, in their righteous haste to fix the world, don't wind up ending the world instead.

The BIS *Green Swan* book winds up being something of a mixed bag. It warns the financial elites to proceed carefully, but encourages them to proceed with haste nonetheless.

On March 20, 2020, just as the coronavirus pandemic was beginning to take its toll on the global economy, the ECB released its "guide on climate-related and environmental risks" and opened up a six-month comment period. The purpose of the guide is "to raise industry awareness of climate-related and environmental risks and to improve the management of such risks" and, more importantly, to serve as a notice to banks that they "are expected to assess whether their current practices are safe and prudent in the light of the expectations and, if necessary, to start adapting them."[92]

As for the Fed, recall that its hands are tied as per Glenn Rudebusch's lament that "by law" it "can only purchase government or government agency debt."

There's only one catch.

As of March 23, 2020, that's not really the case. The Primary Market Corporate Credit Facility (PMCCF) and the Secondary Market Corporate Credit Facility (SMCCF) allow the Fed to lend directly to corporations, that is, to buy existing corporate bonds and corporate-bond Exchange Traded Funds. To reiterate: In 2019, the only barrier to the Fed getting involved more deeply in climate change was its inability to purchase corporate debt. And that is no longer the case.

And the best part? These are the Fed lending programs that are overseen and managed by Larry Fink and BlackRock.

CHAPTER 9

THE PLAYERS, PART TWO: ON THE RIGHT

As noted above, this chapter will be much, much shorter than the last one. That's because, in the battle over capital markets and corporate America more generally, the forces on the Left, the forces advocating for the politicization of business, are far more numerous, far better organized, far better funded, and far more combative than those fighting for depoliticization. It is, in part, simply the case that a call to maintain the status quo or return to the status quo ante will be greeted less enthusiastically than will a call to action, a call for change. Nothing attracts a following like the promise of a revolution, while nothing invites apathy like the promise of "more of the same!"

Nevertheless, those who fight to depoliticize capital markets and the corporate world are dedicated and tireless. This entire book is about the effort, undertaken methodically and relentlessly, to undermine and then to capture the cultural institutions of the West. Those who fight in this battlespace to preserve or reinstate the largely apolitical nature of business capitalization understand that, in many ways, they represent the final point of defense against that which the German legal scholar Carl Schmitt called "the total state."

Although the limitations of language have pigeonholed the debate over American business into the usual ideological framework, this current debate—in addition to all of the other debates over the institutions for the transmission of culture—is somewhat misleading. This isn't strictly a Left-Right battle. The combatants don't fall into discrete ideological camps, and the battles aren't necessarily those that pit liberal against conservative, progressive against traditionalist. Instead, this battle is between those who believe that politics is and should be the overriding force in all human interactions and those who believe that politics is just part of the human experience, a part that is best kept as narrow and limited as possible.

Justin Danhof/The National Center for Public Policy Research/The Free Enterprise Project

Among those who favor depoliticizing the capital markets is the National Center for Public Policy Research, which was founded in 1982 by Amy and David Ridenour to provide a free-market research alternative to the usual left-leaning academic-Washington consensus. The Center is, perhaps, best known for is its efforts in opposition to top-down, one-size-fits-all environmental regulation and health care legislation.

In 2007, the Center launched the Free Enterprise Project (FEP) to combat left-wing attempts to pressure and influence corporations and other business actors. Over the past decade, FEP has focused largely, but not exclusively, on shareholder activism by engaging in what it calls "back-to-neutral" activism and what its opponents call "right-wing" activism. The FEP describes itself as "the conservative movement's only full-service shareholder activism and education program" and says that it "annually files more than 90 percent of all right-of-center shareholder resolutions."[1]

This alone serves as an important measure of just how overmatched the right-leaning, pro–free-market activists are in this arena. The FEP is, in fact, the conservative movement's only shareholder activist group. And for most of the last decade, the FEP *was* Justin Danhof. That is to say that since 2012, Danhof has been everything to the FEP: the director, the associate director, the deputy director, the deputy associate director, the research director, the research assistant, the senior analyst, the senior writer, the administrative assistant, and the part-time shopkeeper. He has been a one-man show, in other words, with occasional support from the rest of the National Center.

In her 2017 bestseller *The Intimidation Game: How the Left Is Silencing Free Speech*, Kimberly Strassel, a columnist and editorial board member at the *Wall Street Journal*, wrote, "If you've never been to a corporate shareholder meeting, you've likely never heard of Justin Danhof. If you ever have been to one, you'll likely never forget him."[2] That's both a compliment to Danhof, who is indefatigable, and a commentary on the state of play in the shareholder activist game. It might be an exaggeration to compare Justin to Leonidas at Thermopylae, but only because Leonidas had 299 other Spartans, while Danhof has been almost entirely on his own.

In pre-COVID days, Danhof was both an effective and aggressive activist and a super-frequent flier, spending every proxy season racing around the country to every shareholder meeting he could get to. Whether he had a proposal on the ballot or not, Danhof would show up to press corporate managers on their policies and plans, to force them to justify their actions and intentions, particularly if they were overtly political. And while he remains as effective and aggressive as he has ever been, the first COVID-era proxy season proved challenging for him, as corporate executives were able to ignore him and his questions and were thus able to avoid divulging any information that they might find embarrassing or discomfiting.

Danhof makes the case that the pressure on corporations to get involved politically and to support political causes comes from three directions: from the top down, from the bottom up, and from the outside in. Or to put it another way, pressure sometimes comes from corporate executives who seek to impose their will on others, using shareholder funds to do so. Think here of Larry Fink or Marc Benioff. Pressure also comes, occasionally, from corporate employees, who have personal political predilections that they would like everyone at work to have to share. Finally, pressure comes from outside activists who set out, specifically and intentionally, to exploit the weaknesses inherent in public corporate governance in order to push a political agenda. Again, think here of Mr. Fink or As You Sow or, frankly, any of the other groups detailed in the last, interminably long chapter.

Danhof is equipped to fight the battle against the politicization of business only on this last front, in the shareholder space. In 2020, he and the FEP were able to hire their first reinforcement in the fight, a former law school instructor and policy expert named Scott Shepard, who was brought on as the Project's coordinator and Danhof's partner in the effort to halt the Left's bowdlerization of corporate America's political independence.

Danhof (and now, Shepard as well) has been one of the most vocal and persistent voices in exposing the Eric Holder–inspired effort to alter the corporate interpretation of diversity. While Holder has been pushing the likes of Larry Fink away from the "common sense" diversity principles that Fink himself co-authored just a few years ago, Danhof has been encouraging corporations to embrace the more inclusive "viewpoint" diversity that Fink once advocated.

During the 2019 shareholder season, Danhof put a handful of very large corporations to the test, introducing a "True Diversity" shareholder proposal to be voted on by the shareholders of Amazon, Salesforce, Twitter, Facebook, and Apple. "We believe," the proposal stated, that "a diverse board is a good indicator of sound corporate governance and a well-functioning board. Diversity in board composition is best achieved through highly qualified candidates with a wide range of skills, experience, beliefs, and board independence from management." And that was simply too much for the corporations and the left-wing activists to stomach. Seriously. When he presented his proposal at Amazon's 2019 shareholder meeting, Danhof was, in his own words, "booed and heckled" throughout his presentation. Afterward, he continues, "a representative from Arjuna Capital suggested that I was there to 'protect white males.' Then, after the meeting, a representative from the Nathan Cummings Foundation tracked me down to suggest I should get going so I wouldn't be late for my 'next Klan meeting or book burning.'"[3]

That is the atmosphere Danhof not only endures but embraces, almost entirely alone, as he fights to get politics out of the boardroom, off the proxy statement, and away from business entirely.

ALEC/Bill Meierling/Lisa Nelson

As Leon Trotsky famously said, "You may not be interested in war, but war is interested in you." The people at ALEC—the American Legislative Exchange Council—know all too well that this adage applies to political warfare as well.

ALEC defines itself as "America's largest nonpartisan, voluntary membership organization of state legislators dedicated to the principles of limited government, free markets and federalism," and claims that "nearly one-quarter of the country's state legislators and stakeholders from across the policy spectrum" are members.[4]

What ALEC does is provide a forum for legislators and private-sector organizations to work together to develop ideas that can be translated into government solutions and partnerships that actually work. It works with its public- and private-sector members to draft, study, and advance "model" legislation. Since its founding in the early 1970s by Paul Weyrich, ALEC has been among the most successful right-of-center organizations in Washington, developing countless pieces of model legislation and influencing some of the most prominent names in the conservative movement. All of which explains why it *had* to be destroyed.

Indeed, in an April 9, 2019 article, USAToday not only quoted former Speaker of the House Newt Gingrich calling ALEC "'the most effective organization' at spreading conservatism and federalism to state lawmakers," but also cited the results of a study demonstrating what Gingrich meant.[5] According to the paper, in a joint investigation with *The Arizona Republic* and the Center for Public Integrity, it discovered that some 10,000 model-legislation bills were introduced in the 50 state legislatures between 2010 and 2018. Of those, 2,900 (or, roughly, 29%) were ALEC model bills. Moreover, more than 600 of those bills were enacted into law. ALEC's success is both impressive and extremely frustrating for its political opponents.

In 2011 *The Nation*, a far-left political magazine, and the George Soros–funded Center for Media and Democracy embarked on a campaign to expose and discredit ALEC. The campaign didn't go all that well until one fateful day in February 2012. On February 26, a 17-year-old African American man named Trayvon Martin was shot and killed by a neighborhood watch volunteer in Sanford, Florida.

The shooter, George Zimmerman, never invoked Florida's "Stand Your Ground" law in his defense of his actions and, indeed, waived his pre-trial Stand Your Ground hearing. And even if he had, Stand Your Ground was a law that was developed in Florida and brought to ALEC from there, not the other way around. Nevertheless, Martin's killing and the liberal Left's attempts to blame Stand Your Ground for it gave the ALEC-haters an opportunity to exploit a tragedy to exact some revenge against the organization for having been so successful. As Kimberly Strassel put it, "The sadness" surrounding the death of a young man "quickly gave way to outrage, and then to something appallingly cynical."[6] Not only was it cynical, but it was, frankly, appalling as well. Strassel continued, "In an interview with Bloomberg in May 2012, Common Cause spokeswoman Mary Boyle explained that her group had been waiting for months for the right moment to file a complaint with the IRS to strip ALEC of its nonprofit status. 'The Trayvon Martin thing was like a gift,' she said, in an extraordinary, if horrifying, moment of honesty."[7]

Gross.

The left-wing activist core got to work, not merely discrediting ALEC but pressuring all of its corporate sponsors and partners to end their relationship with the organization as well. Color of Change, an activist group co-founded by former Obama administration official Van Jones, started a pressure campaign against all the companies that had made the mistake of advertising their support for ALEC. Coca-Cola, Walmart, McDonald's, PepsiCo, Proctor and Gamble, Wendy's, Kraft, Amazon, and on and on the list went. And Color of Change went after them all. And when it was over, they—plus as many as one hundred other corporate sponsors—had all ditched ALEC because they couldn't afford to be associated with the group that the Left insisted was responsible for killing Trayvon Martin.

The activists on the Left had taken the Trayvon Martin killing and had, in turn, nearly killed ALEC. But they didn't kill it. They left it alive, although barely breathing. To save itself and rebuild its public image, ALEC turned to veteran PR professional Bill Meierling and an erstwhile senior government relations executive for Visa named Lisa Nelson. Together, Meierling and Nelson went on the offensive and started fighting back against those who were lying about ALEC and intimidating its corporate sponsors.

The activist Left did significant damage to ALEC, but in the process, it created a new evangelical organization, one dedicated—in addition to all of its other endeavors—to exposing the Left's intimidation tactics, particularly to corporate America. In response to a string of aggressive and dishonest campaigns launched against it and against its corporate partners, ALEC, and especially Bill Meierling, have become activists in their own right, working to teach corporate executives to resist political intimidation and unmasking the bullies of the anti-corporate Left.

The Capital Research Center (CRC)

CRC is a nonpartisan, independent nonprofit, founded in 1984 "to examine how foundations, charities, and other nonprofits spend money and get involved in politics and advocacy, often in ways that donors never intended and would find abhorrent." Given this, CRC is an important ally in the battles against the politicization of almost anything. And capital markets are no exception.

CRC's InfluenceWatch project is an invaluable resource to anyone—Left, Right, center, or otherwise—who is interested in knowing the individuals and organizations involved in influencing public policy issues, including public policy issues in the business/capital markets space. As CRC puts it, it "conceived of this project after identifying a need for more fact-based, accurate descriptions of all of the various influencers" in the policy arena. In so doing, it has made itself a significant and important influencer in its own right.

Omaha

It's not often that the political Right has much cause to celebrate the Oracle of Omaha, Warren Buffett, but it can celebrate him here, on the matter of the politicization of corporate America. Buffett, who is nearly universally known for his very outspoken center-left positions on a variety of issues, most notably taxes, has been equally outspoken in his belief that corporations belong to their shareholders and that using corporate funds for political purposes is unwise.

In an April 2019 interview with the *Financial Times*, Buffett expressed his frustration and annoyance with CEOs and asset managers who use their positions to advance their own political ends. "It was wrong," he said during an interview with the *Times*, "for companies to impose their views of 'doing good' on society. What made them think they knew better?" He continued, "This is the shareholders' money.

Many corporate managers deplore governmental allocation of the taxpayer's dollar, but embrace enthusiastically their own allocation of the shareholder's dollar."[8]

With respect to Berkshire Hathaway's holdings in coal, he added, "If people want us to junk our coal plants, either our shareholders or the consumer is going to pay for it." And Warren Buffett didn't get to be Warren Buffett by screwing over his shareholders.[9]

In the same *Financial Times* interview, Buffett addressed—or avoided addressing, more accurately—questions about the succession plans at Berkshire Hathaway. Who will run Berkshire Hathaway once the great guru is no longer able or willing, the *Financial Times* wanted to know—everyone wants to know.[10] Buffett didn't answer, however, because he hates the question. It is a legitimate concern, however. Buffett turned 90 on August 30, 2020, and someone will, eventually, have to take over for him.

Once upon a time, the man who was expected to do so was Buffett's fellow native Omahan, David Sokol, a structural engineer who made his name in the investment business running MidAmerican Energy, a Berkshire subsidiary, and rescuing two other failing subsidiaries, Johns Manville and NetJets. Sokol left Berkshire in 2011 and today is the chairman of Atlas Corp. and the owner of Teton Capital, a private equity firm. In April 2020, Mr. Sokol authored an open letter to BlackRock CEO Larry Fink that was co-signed by thirty CEOs or corporate executives, taking Fink to task for his decision to use BlackRock to engage in political activism. Sokol wrote the following, fully embracing the original descriptive and instrumental stakeholder models and rejecting the normative version:

> Those of us who have run businesses, or who DO run businesses, know that being shareholder-focused entails a great deal more than our critics pretend. Being a manager or a director of a shareholder-focused company means balancing the needs of various constituencies, including: customers; employees; equity and debt investors, government agencies; and members of the local community. A *successful* business must harmonize the differing and often competing requirements of these constituencies, delivering value and consistency to customers and a productive and safe work environment for employees, all while meeting

federal, state, local regulatory requirements and maintaining a positive presence in the community.

Additionally, we note that most American corporations are already, as practicable, quite forward-looking and concerned with long-term issues and prospects. As such, they strive not merely to meet, but to exceed environmental and other regulatory demands. The effective and profitable deployment of capital in our current regulatory environment is difficult enough. Adding another layer of risk to that decision-making process, thereby penalizing companies that are already going *above and beyond*, would be costly, destructive and, frankly, unfair.[11]

The list of those fighting to prevent the politicization of markets and business includes a handful of others, of course, although in truth, this is the core of the "resistance." Buffett and Sokol are asset managers, who focus more on managing assets and delivering for their clients than on involving themselves in inside-baseball politicized investment skirmishes. That means that the sum of genuine activists working to save American business from the fate suffered by the other American social and cultural institutions comes down to a very small handful of people.

CHAPTER 10

THE WORLD'S BIGGEST CORPORATION: ROTTEN TO THE CORE?

O n June 1, 2020, Apple Inc. CEO Tim Cook sent a memo to his employees, addressing the issue of racism in the United States in the wake of the death of George Floyd. Floyd, recall, had been killed while being subdued by police officers in Minneapolis, Minnesota, and his death sparked national and international outrage. And Tim Cook wanted his employees to know that he, too, was upset. "At Apple," Cook declared, "our mission has and always will be to create technology that empowers people to change the world for the better. We've always drawn strength from our diversity, welcomed people from every walk of life to our stores around the world, and strived to build an Apple that is inclusive of everyone."[1]

Cook continued, saying that Apple would make donations to several different groups, including "the Equal Justice Initiative, a non-profit committed to challenging racial injustice, ending mass incarceration, and protecting the human rights of the most vulnerable people in American society." He concluded by insisting that "With every breath we take, we must commit to being that change, and to creating a better, more just world for everyone."[2]

All of these are, of course, noble sentiments, largely inarguable declarations of solidarity and concern at a time of trouble. But then, this wasn't Tim Cook's first foray into the realms of politics and public morality. Indeed, in many ways, Cook has distinguished himself from his predecessor, Apple founder Steve Jobs, by being outspoken on social issues and by reinventing Apple not as a technology pioneer but as a pioneer for social and political justice. In 2015, Cook, who is gay, used his platform as the CEO of the biggest company in the world (by market capitalization) to address matters he deemed unjust. In a March 29, 2015 op-ed for the *Washington Post*, Cook sharply rebuked state legislators who supported bills that purported to protect religious liberty but were, in Cook's eyes, blatant efforts to discriminate against the LGBTQ community. Most significantly, Cook made it clear that he was not writing about his personal beliefs or his personal thoughts on the legislation, but that he spoke for the company. "That's why," he wrote, "*on behalf of Apple,* I'm standing up to oppose this new wave of legislation [emphasis added]."[3]

In the January-February 2018 edition of the *Harvard Business Review*, Aaron Chatterji and Michael Toffel, business school professors at Harvard and Duke, respectively, discussed the rise of the new "CEO activists" and suggested that Cook was in a unique position. Apple products are particularly "sticky," they noted, meaning that consumers who love Apple will continue to love Apple and aren't going to abandon the brand because they dislike something the CEO says or does.[4] The "stickiness" of the Apple consumers' loyalty gives Cook the leeway to be more open and assertive about his social and political beliefs. Cook seemed set, from his very start, to put their hypothesis to the test.

Apple is one of the ESG movement's darlings. At the end of 2019, Apple was the single largest position BlackRock held. Moreover, it was one of the top five companies held by all actively managed ESG equity portfolios.[5] Cook and Apple have repeatedly filed amicus briefs with the U.S. Supreme Court advocating on behalf of DACA (Deferred Action for Childhood Arrivals) legislation.[6] After the George Floyd protests, Cook announced that he would use $100 million of shareholder funds to pursue the "unfinished work of racial justice and equality" by establishing "Apple's Racial Equity and Justice Initiative."[7]

Most significantly, Cook and Apple have been among the most aggressive companies in advocating for a "carbon-free" future. Indeed, nearly a decade ago, Apple pledged to be carbon-neutral and, moreover, to get *all* of its energy from renewable sources. In 2018, Cook and Apple celebrated achieving that goal, proudly proclaiming that all of its data centers and retail operations were operating exclusively on renewable energy. Hooray!

There was only one catch. Roughly three-quarters of the energy necessary to produce, transport, and sell Apple products is actually used not by Apple, but by its contractors. And those contractors were not and are not using renewables. In April 2019, Apple announced that forty-four of its contractors—most located in China—had agreed to follow Apple's lead and transition to renewables.[8] And while that's all well and good, independent environmental groups have suggested that Apple's claims amount to "greenwashing," which is to say the pretense of environmental friendliness. In a report that coincided with Apple's 2019 announcement, Greenpeace East Asia gave Apple's contractor partners generally poor grades. Hon Hai/Foxconn, which manufactures iPhones for Apple, received a grade of D-, the lowest possible score. Taiwan semiconductor TSMC received a much better grade, B-, but Greenpeace noted that the higher score was mostly due to transparency and that the company still only "powered 5.4% of its operations with renewables."[9]

In truth, Apple's environmental record is complicated—far more complicated than the company or its ESG backers would care to admit. Ethical Consumer, a Manchester, England–based consumer watchdog group that has rated companies for their behaviors since 1989 and publishes a bi-monthly eponymous print magazine, has been among Apple's most strident critics. "Apple," the organization wrote, "received Ethical Consumer's worst rating for environmental reporting in 2019."[10] Note that Ethical Consumer doesn't say that Apple is rated poorly for its environmental behavior, only that its reporting is poor, which suggests that its claims of transparency are not especially accurate. Ethical Consumer also noted that "In 2018, Apple was fined £10 million by the Italian authorities for 'planned obsolescence' built into their smartphones. Furthermore in the US, Apple lobbied a right to repair bill which helped to cause its being pulled. As a result, Apple can be seen as part of the problem of toxic e-waste."[11]

Planned obsolescence is a consistent case made against Apple, largely because building Apple's products requires the use of considerable natural resources, chief among them being cobalt. Lithium-ion batteries are built using cobalt, and 60 percent of the world's cobalt comes from the Democratic Republic of Congo (DRC). Needless to say, neither the government of the DRC nor its primarily Chinese importers are especially concerned about labor laws or practices. In December 2019, Apple was one of five American companies named in a lawsuit filed by International Rights Advocates, a Washington, DC–based human rights law firm, on behalf of fourteen parents and children from the DRC. According to Manchester's *Guardian* newspaper, "The lawsuit, which is the result of field research conducted by antislavery economist Siddharth Kara, accuses the companies of aiding and abetting in the death and serious injury of children who they claim were working in cobalt mines in their supply chain."[12] According to the suit, the children were working illegally for the British mining company Glencore. Glencore sold all its cobalt to Umicore, a Belgian company, which then supplied "battery-grade cobalt to Apple, Google, Tesla, Microsoft and Dell."[13] Among the contentions in the suit was the claim that Apple et al. knew that their cobalt was coming from mines using child labor.

The DRC lawsuit is hardly the first time Apple has been accused of profiting from child labor. Apple has admitted several times to "discovering" that some of its contractors use child labor—defined as employees under 16 years old. Generally, the company blames the problem on the contractor and promises to do better next time.

Sometimes, however, doing better next time can't erase the horrors of the working conditions in Apple's manufacturing plants. The company that claims to want to create "a better, more just world for everyone" has a long and sordid history of profiting from grotesque labor practices. In 2017, the journalist Brian Merchant published a book called *The One Device: The Secret History of the iPhone*. It is worth quoting from at length, given the shocking nature of what Merchant found at Apple's Foxconn iPhone factory at Longhua:

> Foxconn's enormous Longhua plant is a major manufacturer of Apple products. It might be the best-known factory in the world; it might also be among the most secretive and sealed-off. Security guards man each of the entry points. Employees can't get in without swiping an ID card; drivers entering with delivery trucks are subject to fingerprint scans. A Reuters journalist was once dragged out of a car and beaten for taking photos from outside the factory walls. The warning signs outside—"This factory area is legally established with state approval. Unauthorised trespassing is prohibited. Offenders will be sent to

police for prosecution!"—are more aggressive than those outside many Chinese military compounds....

Foxconn is the single largest employer in mainland China; there are 1.3 million people on its payroll. Worldwide, among corporations, only Walmart and McDonald's employ more. As many people work for Foxconn as live in Estonia....

In 2010, Longhua assembly-line workers began killing themselves. Worker after worker threw themselves off the towering dorm buildings, sometimes in broad daylight, in tragic displays of desperation—and in protest at the work conditions inside. There were 18 reported suicide attempts that year alone and 14 confirmed deaths. Twenty more workers were talked down by Foxconn officials....

Foxconn CEO, Terry Gou, had large nets installed outside many of the buildings to catch falling bodies. The company hired counsellors and workers were made to sign pledges stating they would not attempt to kill themselves....

This culture of high-stress work, anxiety and humiliation contributes to widespread depression. Xu says there was another suicide a few months ago. He saw it himself. The man was a student who worked on the iPhone assembly line. "Somebody I knew, somebody I saw around the cafeteria," he says. After being publicly scolded by a manager, he got into a quarrel. Company officials called the police, though the worker hadn't been violent, just angry.

"He took it very personally," Xu says, "and he couldn't get through it." Three days later, he jumped out of a ninth-story window.

So why didn't the incident get any media coverage? I ask. Xu and his friend look at each other and shrug. "Here someone dies, one day later the whole thing doesn't exist," his friend says....[14]

The Longhua factory complex was built exclusively for Foxconn and exclusively to work on Apple products. Some other products may be made there now, but at the start, it was nothing but Apple. And from Apple's perspective, one of the greatest advantages of Longhua is the plausible deniability it provides. Apple is constantly accused of and, in Europe, fined for tax avoidance. But the company insists that it pays all its taxes and complies with all relevant tax laws. And that's where Longhua is important. The factory, you see, is not technically in China. Rather, it is in a "bonded zone," which the Chinese government officially recognizes as "foreign territory." Apple imports all of the components and raw materials for its products into the bonded zone, with no taxes or import duties. Apple "buys" the finished products (mostly iPhones) from Foxconn in the bonded zone and then assigns the products and the profits to various subsidiaries in tax havens around the world, thus avoiding massive amounts of taxation on those profits as well.[15]

Thanks to this perfectly "legal" tax strategy, Apple has made a mint that it has avoided paying any taxes on whatsoever. According to a 2017 report from the nonprofit, nonpartisan Institute on Taxation and Economic Policy, "Apple has booked $246 billion offshore, a sum greater than any other company's offshore cash pile. It is currently avoiding $76.7 billion in U.S. taxes on these earnings."[16]

In the end, most of what happens with Apple cannot be distinguished from what happens with and at the instruction of the Communist Party of China. The CCP needs Apple desperately. As noted above, Foxconn is the third-largest employer in the world. Most of its employees work in China and most of those work for Apple. If Apple were, somehow, to disappear tomorrow, the CCP would have an enormous population of highly skilled, formerly well paid (relatively speaking) people with nothing to do, nowhere to go, and no way to earn a living. A significant majority of these workers are male and most are in their twenties.[17] Given that China already has a serious problem with a gender imbalance unprecedented in world history, some 120 men in their twenties for 100 women of the same age, China would not, *could* not deal with a huge chunk of them suddenly being out of work.

At the same time, though, Apple needs China pretty desperately as well. Not only is China Apple's largest manufacturer, but it is also Apple's second-largest market. Apple's rise to become the biggest and most valuable company in the world was fueled in large part by its growth in China.

The CCP, of course, knows this and knows that Apple can't afford to make it unhappy or upset its leaders. Just since 2017, Apple has, at the request of the CCP: removed the *New York Times* app from the Chinese App Store; removed Skype from the Chinese App Store; removed more than 400 VPN (Virtual Private Network) apps from the App Store; moved all of the user data for its Chinese iCloud users to a server owned by a

Chinese company (in accordance with a new Chinese law); and, most ominously, removed the *Quartz* news app that was covering the Hong Kong protests and blocked an app used by those protesters to organize.

Also, while Tim Cook complains about American states that are grappling with the tradeoffs between religious liberty and the rights of the LGBTQ community, Apple opened its first store in Saudi Arabia—a country in which homosexuality can still be punished by death—in 2018. And while Cook plans to spend $100 million of shareholder funds to address racial inequity and justice in the United States, Apple's patrons in the CCP hold upwards of one million Uighur Muslims in concentration/reeducation camps in what the *Washington Post* rightly calls "cultural genocide."[18]

Tim Cook may well be very concerned about racial and social inequities in the United States. And he may well be very concerned about environmental degradation in the United States. Heaven knows there's much about the country that is imperfect and needs fixing. But either Cook is an enormous hypocrite or...well...there is no other option. Cook is a poseur, and Apple is an ESG fraud.

CHAPTER 11

IS THE HOUSE OF MOUSE CONTAMINATED BY ROTTEN APPLES?

For much of the last two decades, Apple Inc. and the Walt Disney Company have been connected at the hip—or, at the very least, connected at the board of directors. In 2006, Apple founder Steve Jobs sold another of his ventures, Pixar Animation Studios, to Disney. Jobs became the largest single shareholder of Disney in the deal and also joined Disney's board of directors, where he remained until his death in 2011. That same year, Bob Iger, the man who had bought Pixar from Jobs, joined the Apple board, where he would serve until September 2019, when the two companies launched competing streaming video services and Iger felt he could no longer manage the clear conflicts of interest. For many years after her husband's death, Laurene Powell Jobs was the largest single shareholder in Disney, although she cut her share in half a few years ago. Today, the first- and second-largest holders of Disney are Vanguard and BlackRock, respectively. Less than a week after he quit Apple's board, Iger said that if his friend Steve Jobs had lived, it is quite possible that Disney and Apple could have merged to form a monster tech and media company.

Connected at the hip, in other words.

By all accounts, Bob Iger is a nice man, maybe the nicest big-time CEO around. In a long, fawning profile in 2019, *New York Times* columnist Maureen Dowd—the woman Monica Lewinsky called "the queen of mean"—referred to Iger as "Hollywood's nicest CEO."[1] And almost no one disagrees with her. After the constant drama of the Michael Eisner era at Disney, which ended in 2005, Iger was, for many, a welcome change. Whereas Eisner was volatile and dramatic, Iger was calm and even-tempered. Moreover, Iger was a visionary. His acquisitions of Marvel Entertainment in 2009 and LucasFilm Ltd—including Lucas's Star Wars franchise—in 2012 have made Iger Hollywood's most successful CEO as well.

For years, Disney has been among the most liked and most respected name brands in American business. When it comes to brand image or "corporate social responsibility" measures, Disney is almost always among the top five or six companies in the world. Disney sells an image— "the Happiest Place on Earth," "Find your happily ever after," etc.—that evokes what is best about the country, about its history, and the idea that anything can happen "when you wish upon a star." Disney's image is about as wholesome and wonderful and quaintly dutiful as it gets.

Or at least it is on the surface.

In addition to the Jobs-Iger connection, Disney and Apple share a few other things in common. For starters, both their CEOs are interested in politics and are not afraid to put their companies' reputations on the line in pursuit of their political ends. Additionally, both men are multi-centi-millionaires who have become rich beyond the dreams of avarice as managers of companies that someone else built and someone else initially capitalized. Finally, both men are deeply and inextricably linked—by their own choice and their own business strategies—to the Chinese Communist Party. Iger's position vis-à-vis China is stronger than Cook's, but you'd probably never guess that from Iger's actions.

The first signs of trouble at the House of Mouse emerged in late 2015, when *Star Wars: The Force Awakens* was set to open in China, and observers noticed something strange about the movie posters created specifically for the Chinese market: John Boyega—who is African American—was featured prominently on the regular poster but was minimized on the Chinese version. And all the other minority actors were removed from the Chinese poster altogether.[2] The following year, Disney released Marvel's *Doctor Strange*, and the character the Ancient One, who, in the comic book, is a Tibetan monk, was played by British actress Tilda Swinton. When asked about the discrepancy between the comic and the movie, screenwriter C. Robert Cargill said, "He originates from Tibet. So if you acknowledge that Tibet is a place and that he's Tibetan, you risk alienating one billion people who think that that's bulls—t and risk the Chinese government going, 'Hey, you know one of the biggest film-watching countries in the world? We're not going to show your movie because you decided to get political."[3]

While he was kowtowing to China on Tibet and minorities, Iger was getting political at home—in Georgia first and then in North Carolina. In early 2016, the Georgia legislature passed a "religious liberty" bill that was controversial and raised the hackles of various gay rights advocacy groups. Disney and Iger led the charge to block the bill by threatening to boycott the state if it was enacted. And why should Georgia care what Disney thinks? Georgia just happens to be home to the largest film production industry in the United States, largely because of incredibly generous tax breaks offered by the state to film companies, beginning in 2002 and strengthened in 2008. Filmmaking has helped make Georgia one of the economic powerhouses of the New South, and Disney is one of its best customers. But Iger and Disney didn't like what the elected representatives of the people of Georgia believed, so they stomped their mouse-shaped feet and demanded satisfaction. They received that satisfaction just a few weeks later, when Georgia's governor, Republican Nathan Deal, announced that he would veto the bill to spare his state the economic consequences of the boycott.

Deal's position was precarious, and his acquiescence was, therefore, understandable. In so doing, however, he emboldened the likes of Disney to threaten those who disagreed with them politically with economic ruin. Later that same year, Iger and Disney jumped into the political fray once more, signing on to the threatened boycott of North Carolina over its controversial bathroom bill, known as HB2. And while Disney and the rest didn't "win" that battle in the sense that they forced state legislators not to pass or to repeal the bill, they did ensure that the people of North Carolina lost big time, creating considerable economic hardship for the state, just as promised.

Again, while Disney was flexing its political muscles at home, Bob Iger was flexing his neck to bow before Chinese President Xi Jinping in an unusual meeting between the two at the Great Hall of the People in Beijing. Iger and Disney were, at the time, about six weeks away from their biggest venture in some time, the opening of the Shanghai Disney Resort. In an interview the day after opening the park, Iger made it clear that this was a huge deal for him and the company. "This is, I think, a great market for Disney and a growth market as well. Obviously the size of the market, the number of people, is another reason, but, and this is an extremely [big] step—or the biggest step, actually—that we've ever taken anywhere to grow in a market....We continue to grow our motion picture business. So far, most of that has been exporting films that we make in other parts of the world into China; that's delivered great growth. China is now the No. 2 movie market in the world. We also plan to make Disney movies here; we've actually started that process."

In sum, then, Disney, like Apple, needs China.

Over the course of the next couple of years, Iger continued to wow Disney shareholders with the profits the company made, while the board of directors continued to pay Iger better than any CEO in the country. In 2018, Iger's total compensation was over $65 million, which drew the ire of more than a few shareholders, including, famously, that of Abigail Disney, a granddaughter of the company co-founder Roy Disney. Ms. Disney wrote op-eds and testified before the California legislature about the obscenity of Iger's pay package.

Meanwhile, Xi Jinping grew tired of being told that he looks like Winnie the Pooh and had the character banned from social media in China. More damagingly, China banned the Disney film *Christopher Robin*, which reimagined Pooh and company interacting with live-action actors. Iger didn't bat an eyelash.

In 2019, after Iger had finally put to bed the rumors that he would run for the Democratic presidential nomination and the chance to take on Donald Trump, he and Disney nevertheless saw another opportunity to flex their political muscle at home. The elected representatives of the people of Georgia again grew a little too big for their britches and again threatened to enact a law Bob Iger did not like, this time one that banned abortions after six weeks, which is when a fetal heartbeat can generally be heard. Iger again joined the planned boycott of Georgia, saying that he didn't think it would be "practical" for Disney to continue to shoot in Georgia if the state enacted the bill.[4] Disney had made the highest-grossing film of 2019—*Avengers: Endgame*—and the two highest-grossing films of 2018—*Avengers: Infinity War* and *Black Panther*—in Georgia, so Iger's threats were not idle. He promised serious economic consequences for the people of Georgia, and at least mild economic consequences for Disney shareholders, if the people of Georgia defied his demands. Nevertheless, the bill was passed by the legislature and signed by Governor Brian Kemp. The law is currently in legal limbo, however, awaiting a final court decision on its constitutionality.

There is some profound irony here, given that Mr. Iger does not seem to have any problems doing business in France, the home of Disneyland Paris, despite the fact that France forbids abortions after twelve weeks. A twelve-week ban in the United States—i.e., a ban after the first trimester— would, in practice and in politics, be virtually the same as the Georgia law. And yet that didn't stop Bob Iger from embarking on a $2.5 billion renovation and expansion of his Paris theme park in early 2018.

Fortunately for Mr. Iger, the Georgia law was not the only political kerfuffle of 2019, which meant that he would have a chance to redeem himself before year's end. Unfortunately, he did not redeem himself, and, indeed, made matters worse.

In October, Daryl Morey, the general manager of the NBA's Houston Rockets, tweeted an image that read "Fight for Freedom. Stand with Hong Kong." Because the Chinese government is incapable of tolerating even the mildest criticism, and because the NBA—like Disney and Apple— has sold its soul to the CCP for a bag of money, Morey's tweet didn't go over all that well in China or in the league offices. NBA commissioner Adam Silver quickly began begging for forgiveness from the CCP and began warning the rest of the league's players, coaches, and executives to keep their mouths shut about Hong Kong. LeBron James, Steve Kerr, and Gregg Popovich, three of the NBA's loudest and most banal social justice warriors, quickly busted out their knee pads so they wouldn't hurt themselves leaping to the floor to grovel before Xi.

Meanwhile, over at ESPN, the world's largest sports network and a Walt Disney Company network, word went forth from management not to discuss the matter of Hong Kong on air. According to *Deadspin*, "Chuck Salituro, the senior news director of ESPN, sent a memo to shows mandating that any discussion of the Daryl Morey story avoid any political discussions about China and Hong Kong, and instead focus on the related basketball issues." Later that month, at the *Wall Street Journal's* Tech Live conference in Laguna Beach, California, Iger was asked about the controversy and adamantly refused to say anything about Hong Kong, much less anything about the CCP and its deadly leaders. "What we learned in the last week—we've learned how complicated this is," he stated. "The biggest learning from that is that caution is imperative. To take a position that could harm our company in some form would be a big mistake. I just don't believe it's something we should engage in in a public manner."

In essence, then, when faced with American political issues that are unlikely to result in anyone, anywhere getting hurt, much less dying, Bob Iger is a full-throated political activist. When faced with the violence and lawlessness of his business partners in Beijing, however, the CEO of Disney is much more reticent to speak, insisting that the whole matter is "complicated."

It's really not all that complicated, of course. It's only complicated if you've bet everything on China and can't afford to lose. In that case, principles and "corporate social responsibility" tend to take a back seat to other, less admirable values.

One should have guessed, in other words, that Bob Iger would follow Tim Cook into the moral morass of the People's Republic of China.

CHAPTER 12

AMAZON, HATE, AND THE POVERTY PALACE

Jeff Bezos, the founder and CEO of Amazon, is a charitable guy. With an estimated fortune of more than $150 billion, he can, of course, afford to be. But still, it's nice when someone with his means is generous with his wealth—not that there has ever been anybody else with his means in the history of the planet. For many years, Bezos wasn't considered particularly charitable and was even thought of as something of a Scrooge. That all changed in 2018, however, when Bezos made a monster pledge of $2 billion to develop and implement education programs for the homeless. Bezos's donations before 2018 would be considered extremely generous if they were made by anyone other than the richest man ever. But, then, everybody's a critic.

Bezos's biggest charitable donations thus far include the following: a 2011 $10 million gift to the Museum of History and Industry in Seattle; a 2011 $15 million donation to the Princeton Neuroscience Institute; a 2012 $2.5 million grant to Washington United for Marriage, which is a same sex marriage advocacy organization; a 2016 $1 million matching gift made to Mary's Place, which serves the homeless; a 2017 $1 million donation to the Reporters Committee for Freedom of the Press; a 2018 $33 million gift to TheDream.us, which provides scholarships to immigrants; a 2018 $10 million contribution to With Honor, a political action committee that works to elect veterans; the 2018 launch of the Bezos Day One Foundation, which started with $97.5 million for homeless families; a 2019 $98.5 million donation to the Bezos Day One Foundation; an April 2020 $100 million donation to Feeding America for the COVID-19 Response Fund;[1] and last, but far from least, the February 2020 launch of the Bezos Earth Fund with a staggering donation of $10 billion to fight climate change.[2] As he launched the latter, Bezos wrote on Instagram: "Climate change is the biggest threat to our planet. I want to work alongside others both to amplify known ways and to explore new ways of fighting the devastating impact of climate change on this planet we all share."[3]

In addition to his own charitable donations—which, obviously, is a long and very left-leaning list—Bezos's company operates the AmazonSmile program. AmazonSmile allows customers to dedicate a portion of their purchases to be donated to the charity of their choice. Over the course of the program's lifetime, Amazon customers have donated some $160 million to charities, including $44 million in fiscal 2018 alone.[4]

Sounds great, right?

The only catch is that Amazon uses information provided by the Southern Poverty Law Center to determine which charities are and are not eligible to receive donations. And the SPLC, in turn, is a deeply political, highly partisan, exceptionally well-funded, and very professional direct-mail scam. The Philanthropy Roundtable once called the SPLC "Hate, Inc.,"[5] which is to say that the organization thrives on—and makes a great deal of money from—convincing people that there are "hate groups" all over the country trying to kill them, steal their stuff, and enslave their children. In truth, however, SPLC is a direct-mail fundraising operation that does a little lawyering on the side. *National Review*'s Kyle Smith once noted that "SPLC, founded by a direct-mail zillionaire named Morris Dees, spends far more on direct-mail fundraising pleas ($10 million) than it ever has on legal services, according to an analysis by Philanthropy Roundtable, and has never passed along more than 31 percent of its funding to charitable programs, sometimes as little as 18 percent."[6]

How much money, exactly, has the organization made? A lot. Under the direction of the now-deposed Morris Dees, the SPLC amassed a fortune, not a small fortune, mind you, but a big, real-life, actual fortune. In April 2019, Tyler O'Neil, a senior editor at *PJ Media* and the author of the SPLC exposé *Making Hate Pay: The Corruption of the Southern Poverty Law Center*, described the organization's war chest this way: "According to the SPLC's tax documents, the organization has $529,801,832 in its endowment, the second year it had more than half a billion dollars on hand. According to an accounting firm's report first publicized by the Washington Free Beacon's Joe Schoffstall, the SPLC has $570 million in assets, including the $41 million in its action fund launched just last year. Annual contributions in 2019 stood at $97 million, down from the $132 million it reported in October 2017....Most astonishingly, the SPLC reported $162 million in offshore accounts in the Cayman Islands."[7]

All of that said, the biggest problem with the SPLC isn't that it makes or has a lot of money. The biggest problem isn't even that it raises that money through less-than-honest means. (That *is* a problem, just not the relevant problem for this book.) No, the biggest problem with the SPLC is that singles out, smears, and then effectively defunds conservative and traditional religious organizations in the name of fighting "hate." And because of AmazonSmile, it does so, in part, with Jeff Bezos's blessing.

Morris Dees, the co-founder and best-known member of the organization, was fired in 2019 amid widespread accusations of racial disparities and sexual harassment, not only by him but up and down the organization as well.[8] Just after Dees was fired, Bob Moser, an award-winning left-wing writer for *The Nation, Rolling Stone*, and *The New Yorker*, among others, penned a long and brutal takedown of the SPLC based in large part on his own recollections, having worked for the Center in the early 2000s. He painted a picture of a truly dysfunctionally functional organization, an operation that did exactly what it was set up to do—bilk guilty white northerners out of as much money as possible, while appearing to fight "hate" and mete out righteous punishment to evildoers—but did so in the most grievous and ugly ways. Moser described the SPLC's much-ballyhooed hate group list as "a masterstroke of Dees's marketing talents,"[9] in that it convinces countless gullible journalists to provide the Center immeasurable free publicity by recounting the "rising tide of hate" and referring directly to the Center and its list—every year, year after year.

In the March 2019 edition of the left-of-center *Current Affairs* magazine, Nathan Robinson, the magazine's editor-in-chief, described the SPLC's "hate list" as "everything that is wrong with liberalism."[10] He argued that "the biggest problem with the hate map, though, is that it's an outright fraud," and that "the whole thing is a willful deception designed to scare older liberals into writing checks to the SPLC."[11]

Robinson noted that the Center doesn't "actually link to or provide details about many of the groups it profiles, perhaps because this would reveal what a joke many of them are."[12]

Unfortunately, when it isn't fighting jokes and scaring old white liberals, the SPLC does serious damage to mainstream conservatives and conservative organizations, like Charles Murray, the Alliance for Defending Freedom, and Daniel Pipes and the Middle East Forum. It attacks and endangers Muslim reformers like Maajid Nawaz (to whom the SPLC lost a $4 million defamation lawsuit). And it maligns traditional Christian organizations like the Family Research Council. Indeed, in 2012, a man named Floyd Lee Corkins, who later admitted that he had been radicalized by the SPLC's hate list, attacked the Family Research Council headquarters in Washington and brought a bag of Chick-fil-A sandwiches with him, hoping to kill "haters" and then "smear" Christian-radical chicken sandwiches in their faces. Corkins is now serving twenty-five years in federal prison.

So, what happens to an Amazon customer who tries to sign up for AmazonSmile and direct his donation to the Middle East Forum or ACT for America? He or she receives a response from Amazon that reads: "The AmazonSmile Participation Agreement states that certain categories of organizations are not eligible to participate in AmazonSmile. We rely on the Southern Poverty Law Center to determine which charities are in certain ineligible categories. You have been excluded from the AmazonSmile program because the Southern Poverty Law Center lists [insert organization name here] in an ineligible category." If the SPLC, a fear-mongering direct-mail scam with a history of sexual harassment and racial bias, deems a charity unworthy, then Amazon itself deems the charity unworthy.[13]

And the best part? Of all the charities and nonprofits in the world, SPLC is #33 on the list of biggest beneficiaries of the AmazonSmile program, taking in at least $37,739.17.[14]

At the 2020 Amazon shareholder meeting, Justin Danhof, the director of the Free Enterprise Project (see Chapter 9), had a proposal on the proxy statement, one in which he suggested that continued partnership with the SPLC posed a reputational risk to Amazon and, therefore, the company should disassociate itself from the Center. Amazon's board of directors recommended voting against Danhof's proposal, and CEO

Jeff Bezos dodged Danhof's question about the SPLC and viewpoint diversity.

It is worth noting here that, in addition to his stake in Amazon, Jeff Bezos owns the *Washington Post,* one of the nation's leading left-of-center newspapers and the paper that, in the 1990s, infamously called conservative Christians—the type of people whom the SPLC often targets— "poorly educated and easily led."

In the wake of the death of George Floyd and the subsequent protests, Bezos said that Amazon would donate $10 million to "social justice organizations" like Black Lives Matter in order to combat "racism and the disproportionate risk that Black people face in our law enforcement and justice systems."[15] Note that this donation was from Amazon and its shareholders, not from Bezos personally.

It is also worth noting that the Black Lives Matter protests were, at times, overtaken by violence, rioting, and looting. According to both the federal government and media observers, one of the reasons these protests turned violent and ugly was the presence of Antifa agitators in the crowd, who were more interested in fomenting chaos and anarchy than in finding just and equitable solutions to the problems between law enforcement and the black community. And according to Tyler O'Neil, who, recall, has written the definitive book on the SPLC, "journalists with HuffPost, *The Guardian,* and the Southern Poverty Law Center (SPLC) have maintained connections with Antifa activists, a new report revealed."[16] If true, that would put Amazon in league with an organization that is in close contact with the radical fringe group that has been trying to co-opt the Black Lives Matter energy and frustration and use it to advance its own considerably less noble ends. Talk about reputational risk.

It should not go unmentioned that Amazon, with its clean and wholesome image, has long been accused by former employees of treating workers poorly, with little concern for their health or well-being. Amid the coronavirus pandemic in 2020, Amazon was accused of firing senior employees who complained about the conditions in the company's warehouses. After those terminations, a senior engineer and vice president of the company named Tim Bray resigned from the company in protest, saying that he felt he had no choice, and that staying on the job "would have meant, in effect, signing off on actions I despised."[17]

Finally, the chief spokesman for Amazon is a man named Jay Carney. If that name sounds familiar, that's because he served in the same position in the Obama White House. In October 2019, Carney told those gathered at a tech conference in Seattle that "Virtually with no exception, everyone I dealt with in [the Clinton and Obama] administrations, whether I personally agreed or disagreed with what they thought were the right policy decisions or the right way to approach things, I never doubted that they were patriots. I don't feel that way now." When President Trump retweeted his comments, Carney tried, unsuccessfully, to walk them back and to draw a distinction between his personal feelings and his official positions as the spokesman for Amazon.[18] Again, reputational risk.

IN CONCLUSION

Of all the philosophers and moral theorists cited in this book, ostensibly about the practical and functional application of business-funding mechanisms—and there are many, mostly Germans, ranging from Marx to Nietzsche to von Schmoller to Horkheimer to Marcuse—it is quite possible that the most important and the most relevant philosopher of them all is another German, one not yet mentioned.

Carl Schmitt was a brilliant legal scholar in the Weimar era who was also what one might call a "case in point." One of Schmitt's primary concerns was what he saw as the blurring of the line that separated the state from society. This, he argued, fostered a permanent state of argument, hostility, and change—in the political realm. Looking at the Western world after the Great War, Schmitt saw that liberal democracy provided man with a nearly unlimited variety of partisan and ideological viewpoints. Each of these was displeased with something in society, saw some flaw that desperately needed fixing. And so, each promised the means to fix that which was broken, to harness the power of the state to deliver its favored end or to destroy the state if it prevented the actualization of that end. Schmitt called this the "total state," which he defined as a society that "no longer knows anything absolutely nonpolitical."

Schmitt believed that, traditionally, Western societies were not like this, that the state and therefore politics applied only to a very narrow band of public matters—land, trade, state finances, and family ties, for example. The new liberal democracies, the new "total state" was defined by its interest and participation in every aspect of civic life, from the social to the economic, from the personal to the religious.

Like Max Weber, who was twenty-five years his senior, Schmitt intended his observations to be understood as descriptive, not prescriptive, which is to say that he believed he was describing how politics is or how it functions in practice, rather than explaining what he thought politics *should* be or how it *should* function.

Starting from the banal observation that a state needs a sovereign, Schmitt moved on to the slightly less banal idea that a popular (i.e., democratic) sovereign is perfectly adequate in a homogenous state, where all citizens share the same self-identification and many of the same principal interests.

In practice, however, there are no states that possess this homogeneous self-identification, and that means that the political realm becomes a battlefield on which various ideas and beliefs compete for supremacy and on which people and groups come to see others as "friends" or "enemies." Schmitt believed that the distinction between these two, between friend and enemy, is not necessarily defined by traditional dualistic moral concepts like "right and wrong," "good and evil," "beautiful and ugly." Rather, he suggested that the "political enemy" "need not be morally evil or esthetically ugly; he need not appear as an economic competitor, and it may even be advantageous to engage with him in business transactions. But he is nevertheless, the other, the stranger... each participant is in a position to judge whether the adversary intends to negate his opponent's way of life and therefore must be repulsed or fought in order to preserve one's own form of existence."

What this means, then, is that the divisions in the modern, total state are delineated by the nebulous notion of "values." Values are not the same as traditional moral beliefs, which are rooted in religious teachings. Instead, values depend on self-defined self-interest. And that means that man identifies friends as those who share the same self-interest, and enemies as those who do not.

Schmitt goes on to argue that war among the total states is much different and much more likely to be truly devastating than previous wars. "Such a war," he writes, "is necessarily unusually intense and inhuman because, by transcending the limits of the political framework, it simultaneously degrades the enemy into moral and other categories and is forced to make of him a monster that must not only be defeated but also utterly destroyed." War among men in the total state is total war, one that transcends all shared humanity and all otherwise common characteristics and therefore demands total victory.

One needn't be a German legal theorist to see that this concept of total war in the total state applies beyond the realm of actual, literal war and can be applied to just about any conflict in the total state. "The political" is omnipresent. It dominates every aspect of our lives, just as Schmitt observed and predicted, and it therefore ensures that any disagreement becomes an occasion for total war and the division of all people into combatant groups, friends or enemies.

Part I of this book detailed how the total state came to dominate every aspect of modern life, save one—business and capital markets. It traced the history of the ideas that produced the total politicized state and the application of those ideas to create a total, political societal ethos.

Part II identified the combatants, the friends and enemies, and the techniques utilized in the last battle in this war, the battle to dominate this final sphere of human enterprise and to make it a part of "the political" and a part of the total state as well. The values over which this war is being waged are not only clear and indisputable but are also the defining values of our civilization. And at the risk of being overdramatic, the fate of a civilization may well rest on the outcome of this particular battle, which is precisely why those who would make business and markets part of "the political" are fighting it so totally, so remorselessly.

There is a profound irony here and a profound warning. Carl Schmitt understood that this value development and self-identification would create political disorder. He also explained how order might be restored in such a society, where multiple friend-enemy factions had developed.

Democratic sovereignty necessarily elevates one faction over another. This, in turn, eliminates substantive equality, exacerbates disorder, and calls into question the legitimacy of the sovereign. The only way to remedy all of this, Schmitt argued, and thus to restore order, is to trade sovereign democracy for a sovereign dictator.

Carl Schmitt was a living, breathing oxymoron. He grew frustrated with and tired of trying to rationalize the inefficiencies and ineffectiveness of the Weimar Republic, and so he chose to pledge his allegiance to those who would restore order. And he became "the crown juror of the Third Reich."

By pledging his fidelity to the Nazis, Schmitt both fulfilled his pre-Nazi philosophical theories and, at the same time, sacrificed his personal credibility. He became a significant part of the problem he identified and professed to find intolerable.

Conflict in politics is normal and, in a state in which the people serve as the sovereign, is inevitable. But the knee-jerk demand for order in the face of this conflict is, quite simply, the path to dictatorship and the subjugation of those whose values differ from the majority.

When those who hold the most power in society determine to end conflict by waging total war and destroying those they've identified as enemies, society loses everything, not just its variety but the very mechanism by which variety is created in the first place.

Disorder is uncomfortable. It is messy. It is not always efficient. But it is from disorder that creative destruction springs. The urge to bring order to disorder, to impose constancy on variability, to consolidate values is not just the means by which liberty is killed, it is also the means by which Schumpeter's gale is killed.

The choice here is simple. If we as a civilization allow even the spirit of capitalism to become part of "the political" and part of the total state, then we will have order—for however long that lasts. If we resist the politicization of business and of capital markets, however; if we determine for ourselves that disorder and depoliticization are the preferable options, then we not only preserve liberty but also preserve the spirit of innovation and expression that harnesses liberty to create wealth and prosperity.

It does not matter, in the grand scheme, if the "values" advocated for homogenization of business and markets are reasonable-sounding and bear reassuring names like "pragmatism" or "neopragmatism." All that matters is that this attempt to shift the normative discussion away from the shared morals of our civilization and to the "values" of friend-enemy dichotomy will ultimately destroy everything else in the process.

Depoliticize business.

Depoliticize markets.

Back to neutral.

NOTES

INTRODUCTION

1 Larry Fink, "Sustainability as BlackRock's New Standard for Investing," January 2020, https://www.blackrock.com/corporate/investor-relations/blackrock -client-letter.

2 Chris Flood, "Record Sums Deployed into Sustainable Investment Funds," *Financial Times*, January 19, 2020, https://www.ft.com/content /2a6c38f7-4e4b-411b-b5e6-96b36e597cfc.

3 The Business Roundtable, "Statement on the Purpose of a Corporation," August 19, 2019, https://opportunity.businessroundtable.org/wp-content/uploads /2020/04/BRT-Statement-on-the-Purpose-of-a-Corporation-with-Signatures -Updated-April-2020.pdf.

4 The Business Roundtable, "Business Roundtable Redefines the Purpose of a Corporation to Promote 'An Economy That Serves All Americans'" (press release), August 19, 2019, https://www.businessroundtable.org/business -roundtable-redefines-the-purpose-of-a-corporation-to-promote-an-economy -that-serves-all-americans.

5 Matt Levine, "Maybe CEOs Are Fed Up with Shareholders," *Bloomberg Opinion*, August 19, 2019, https://www.bloomberg.com/opinion/articles/2019-08-19/ maximize-shareholder-value-top-ceos-might-be-opting-out.

CHAPTER 1: TO WHOM DOES WALL STREET BELONG?

1 Kimberly Amadeo, "Stock Market Crash of 1929 Facts, Causes, and Impact," The Balance, April 28, 2020, https://www.thebalance.com/ stock-market-crash-of-1929-causes-effects-and-facts-3305891.

2 Wikipedia, "Song of the South," https://en.wikipedia.org/wiki/Song_of_the _South_(song) (accessed August 1, 2020).

3 Snopes.com, "Was President George H.W. Bush 'Amazed' by a Grocery Scanner?", April 1, 2001, https://www.snopes.com/fact-check /bush-scanner-demonstration/.

4 Stacy Conradt, "Never Forget the Time Dan Quayle Misspelled 'Potato,'" Mentalfloss.com, June 16, 2015, https://www.mentalfloss.com/article/64689 /never-forget-time-dan-quayle-misspelled-potato.

5 Kathleen Elkins, "A brief history of the 401(k), which changed how Americans retire," CNBC.com, January 4, 2017, https://www.cnbc.com/2017/01/04/a-brief -history-of-the-401k-which-changed-how-americans-retire.html.

6 Macrotrends.net, "Dow Jones – DJIA – 100 Year Historical Chart," https:// www.macrotrends.net/1319/dow-jones-100-year-historical-chart (accessed August 1, 2020).

7 Open Secrets.org, "Barack Obama (D), Top Contributors 2008 Cycle," Center for Responsive Politics, https://www.opensecrets.org/pres08/contrib.php?cid =n00009638 (accessed August 1, 2020).

8 Kevin D. Williamson, "Losing Gordon Gecko," *National Review*, March 9, 2009, https://www.nationalreview.com/magazine/2009/03/09/losing -gordon-gekko/.

CHAPTER 2: WILSON, WALDO, AND THE FED

1 Johns Hopkins University, "History and Mission," https://www.jhu.edu/about /history/ (accessed August 1, 2020).

2 Richard T. Ely, "The Next Things in Social Reform," Christian Union (New York), XLIII (April 23, 1891), 531.

3 Richard T. Ely, *The Past and Present of Political Economy* (Baltimore: Johns Hopkins University, 1884), 64, https://library.si.edu/digital-library/book /pastpresentofpolo0oelyr.

4 Richard T. Ely, *Social Aspects of Christianity* (New York: T.Y. Crowell, 1889), 92, 77.

5 Jonah Goldberg, "Richard Ely's Golden Calf," *National Review*, December 31, 2009, https://www.nationalreview.com/magazine/2009/12/31/richard-elys -golden-calf/.

6 *The Papers of Woodrow Wilson* (Princeton: Princeton University Press), vol. 3: 447–48, vol. 4: 628–31.

7 Bruce E. Kaufman, *The Global Evolution of Industrial Relations* (Geneva: International Labour Organization, 2004), 60.

8 Woodrow Wilson, "The Study of Administration," *Political Science Quarterly* 2, no. 2 (1887): 197–222.

9 Henry Cabot Lodge, "Chairman of the Senate Foreign Relations Committee Henry Cabot Lodge, Senate speech opposing the League of Nations, February 28, 1919," Massachusetts Institute of Technology web archives, http://web.mit. edu/21h.102/www/Lodge,%20Opposition%20to%20the%20League%20of%20 Nations.html (accessed August 1, 2020).

10 Wilson, "The Study of Administration," 210.

11 Frank Johnson Goodnow, *The American Conception of Liberty*, Google Books edition, Natural Law, Natural Rights, and American Constitutionalism, July 27,

2010, https://www.nlnrac.org/critics/american-progressivism/primary
-source-documents/american-conception-of-liberty.

12 Leonard D. White, *Introduction to the Study of Public Administration*, revised
edition (Prentice-Hall, 1954), originally published 1926.

13 Patrick Overeem, "Beyond Heterodoxy: Dwight Waldo and the Politics
-Administration Dichotomy," *Public Administration Review* 68, no. 1 (Jan/Feb
2008): 36–45.

14 George Lowery and Dana Cooke, "Dwight Waldo Started It All," *Maxwell
Perspective*, Winter 2019, https://www.maxwell.syr.edu/news/perspective
/dwight-waldo-started-it-all/.

15 Ferdinand Lundberg, *America's 60 Families* (New York: Vanguard Press, 1937),
114.

CHAPTER 3: THE LONG MARCH THROUGH THE INSTITUTIONS

1 Antonio Gramsci, *Selections from the Prison Notebooks* (London: ElecBook,
1999), 23.

2 Malachi Martin, *The Keys of This Blood* (New York: Simon and Schuster, 2008),
244–5.

3 Victor Zitta, *Georg Lukács' Marxism Alienation, Dialectics, Revolution* (Berlin:
Springer, 2013), 106.

4 Max Horkheimer, *Critical Theory* (New York: Continuum Publishing Co.,
1989), 245–6.

5 Jürgen Habermas, *The Philosophical Discourse of Modernity: Twelve Lectures*
(New York: John Wiley & Sons, 2015), 116.

6 Paul Johnson, *Modern Times: A History of the World from the 1920s to the 1980s*
(London: Weidenfeld & Nicolson, 1983), 11.

7 John Maynard Keynes, *Two Memoirs: Dr. Melchior: A Defeated Enemy and My
Early Beliefs* (New York: A.M. Kelley, 1949).

8 Norman Cohn, *The Pursuit of the Millennium: Revolutionary Millenarians and
Mystical Anarchists of the Middle Ages* (London: Secker & Warburg, 1957).

9 Roger Kimball, "Some Perils of Sexual Liberation," *The New Criterion*, January
26, 2005, https://newcriterion.com/blogs/dispatch/some-perils-of-sexual
-liberation.

10 Martin Jay, "Preface to the 1996 Edition," in *The Dialectical Imagination: A
History of the Frankfurt School and the Institute of Social Research* (Berkeley:
University of California Press, 1996), xiv.

11 Thomas Wheatland, *The Frankfurt School in Exile* (Minneapolis: University of
Minnesota Press, 2009), 340, https://www.upress.umn.edu/book-division
/books/the-frankfurt-school-in-exile.

12 Paul Piccone, "Twenty Years of *Telos*," *Telos* 75, Summer 1988: 4.

13 Wheatland, *The Frankfurt School*, 341.

CHAPTER 4: WHERE TWO STREAMS MEET

1 R.W. Puyt, Finn Birger Lie, and F.J. de Graaf, "Contagious ideas and cognitive
artefacts: the SWOT Analysis evolution in business," in BAM2017 Conference
Proceedings, 2–19, https://pure.hva.nl/ws/files/4388766/contribution351_2.pdf,
7.

2   Ibid., 9.

3   Ibid., 11.

4   Ibid., 10.

5   Ibid., 11.

6   Israel Unterman, "American Finance: Three Views of Strategy," *Journal of General Management* 1, no. 3: 39–47 (first published Mar. 1, 1974).

7   William R. Dill, "Public participation in corporate planning—strategic management in a Kibitzer's world," *Long Range Planning* 8, no. 1: 57–63.

8   Mariann Jelinek, *Institutionalizing Innovation: A Study of Organizational Learning Systems* (New York: Praeger, 1979), 139.

9   Thomas Donaldson and Lee E. Preston, "The Stakeholder Theory of the Corporation: Concepts, Evidence, and Implications," *The Academy of Management Review* 20, no. 1 (Jan. 1995): 69–70.

10 Ibid., 70.

11 Ibid.

12 Henry Mintzberg, "The Fall and Rise of Strategic Planning," *Harvard Business Review*, Jan./Feb. 1994, https://hbr.org/1994/01/the-fall-and-rise-of-strategic-planning.

13 R. Edward Freeman et al., *Stakeholder Theory: The State of the Art* (Cambridge: Cambridge University Press, 2010), 52.

14 Ibid., 55.

15 Ibid., 56.

16 Ibid., 57.

17 Donaldson and Preston, "The Stakeholder Theory of the Corporation," 72.

18 Ibid.

19 Ibid.

20 Ibid., 81.

21 Ibid., 74.

22 Ibid.

23 Freeman et al., *Stakeholder Theory*, 72.

24 Jonah Goldberg, *The Tyranny of Clichés: How Liberals Cheat in the War of Ideas* (New York: Sentinel/Penguin Group, 2013), https://www.amazon.com/Tyranny-Clich%C3%A9s-Liberals-Cheat-Ideas/dp/1595231021.

25 John Dewey, "Between Two Worlds," Winter Institute of Arts and Sciences Lecture, March 20, 1944.

26 Roger Kimball, "Sausages, enlightenment, and 'critical thinking,'" PJ Media, June 20, 2008, https://pjmedia.com/rogerkimball/2008/06/20/162-n114913.

27 Felski, Rita, "Critique and the Hermeneutics of Suspicion," *M/C Journal* 15, no. 1 (2012), http://journal.media-culture.org.au/index.php/mcjournal/article/viewArticle/431.

28 Kimball, "Some Perils of Sexual Liberation."

29 John Rawls, *Justice as Fairness: A Restatement*, ed. Erin Kelly (Cambridge, Massachusetts: Belknap Press, 2001), 42–43.

30 Ibid., 138.

31 Youtube.com, "Obama says Constitution is a 'charter of negative liberties,'" https://www.youtube.com/watch?v=gqyY6ax3hc0 (posted November 17, 2016).

CHAPTER 5: FRIEDMAN, SOREL, AND THE HEROIC MYTH

1 Theodore Lowi, *The End of Liberalism: Ideology, Policy, and the Crisis of Public Authority* (New York: W.W. Norton, 1969).

2 Gordon Tullock, "The Welfare Costs of Tariffs, Monopolies, and Theft," *Western Economic Journal* 5, no. 3: 224–32.

3 Anne Krueger, "The Political Economy of the Rent-Seeking Society," *The American Economic Review* 64, no. 3 (June 1974): 291–303.

4 William A. *Niskanen, "Nonmarket Decision Making: The Peculiar Economics of Bureaucracy," The American Economic Review 58, no. 2 (May 1968): 293–305.*

5 *Karl R.* Popper, *Conjectures and Refutations*, 4th ed. (1972, London: Routledge and Keagan Paul), 124.

6 Milton Friedman, "The Social Responsibility of Business Is to Increase Its Profits," *New York Times Magazine*, September 13, 1970, https://web.archive.org/web/20060207060807/https:/www.colorado.edu/studentgroups/libertarians/issues/friedman-soc-resp-business.html.

7 Joseph L. Bower and Lynn S. Paine, "The Error at the Heart of Corporate Leadership," *Harvard Business Review* 95, no. 3 (May–June 2017): 50–60, https://hbr.org/2017/05/managing-for-the-long-term#the-error-at-the-heart-of-corporate-leadership.

8 Michael C. Jensen and William H. Meckling, "Theory of the Firm: Managerial Behavior, Agency Costs and Ownership Structure," Journal of Financial Economics (JFE) 3, no. 4 (1976), https://papers.ssrn.com/sol3/papers.cfm?abstract_id=94043.

9 Michael C. Jensen and Kevin J. Murphy, "CEO Incentives—It's Not How Much You Pay, But How," *Harvard Business Review* 68, no. 3 (May–June 1990): 138–49, https://hbr.org/1990/05/ceo-incentives-its-not-how-much-you-pay-but-how.

10 Steve Denning, "Making Sense of Shareholder Value: 'The World's Dumbest Idea,'" Forbes.com, July 17, 2017, https://www.forbes.com/sites/stevedenning/2017/07/17/making-sense-of-shareholder-value-the-worlds-dumbest-idea/#2887ad362a7e.

11 Francesco Guerrera, "Welch condemns share price focus," *Financial Times*, March 12, 2009, https://www.ft.com/content/294ff1f2-0f27-11de-ba10-0000779fd2ac#axzz1eiLpL2PZ.

12 Jensen and Meckling, "Theory of the Firm," 305.

13 Jensen and Murphy, "CEO Incentives."

14 Donaldson and Preston, "The Stakeholder Theory of the Corporation," 69–70.

15 Saul David Alinsky, *Rules for Radicals* (New York: Random House, 1971), 130.

16 Steve Denning, "The 'Pernicious Nonsense' of Maximizing Shareholder Value," Forbes.com, April 27, 2017, https://www.forbes.com/sites/stevedenning/2017/04/27/harvard-business-review-the-pernicious-nonsense-of-maximizing-shareholder-value/#7294a8e271f0.

17 Georges Sorel, *Reflexions sur la violence*, 2nd ed. (New York: B.W. Huebsch, 1912), 202.

CHAPTER 6: FROM SRI TO ESG

1 John Wesley, *The Use of Money*, republished by Effective Altruism for Christians (eaforchristians.org), translated and abridged by Richard Hall, https://www.eaforchristians.org/john-wesley-the-use-of-money-12/ (posted March 1, 2017).

2 Ross Gittell, Matt Magnusson, and Michael Merenda, *The Sustainable Business Case Book* (Washington, D.C.: Saylor Foundation, 2012), https://saylordotorg.github.io/text_the-sustainable-business-case-book/index.html.

3 Bailard (Capital and Wealth Management), "FROM SRI TO ESG: The Origins of Socially Responsible and Sustainable Investing," Bailard Thought Series, June 2017, https://www.bailard.com/wp-content/uploads/2017/06/Socially -Responsible-Investing-History-Bailard-White-Paper-FNL.pdf?pdf=SRI -Investing-History-White-Paper.

4 "Sullivan Principles," Wikipedia.org, accessed August 1, 2020, https:// en.wikipedia.org/wiki/Sullivan_principles#cite_note-Sullivan1977-1.

5 Gregory Gethard, "Protest Divestment and the End of Apartheid," Investopedia, January 25, 2019, https://www.investopedia.com/articles /economics/08/protest-divestment-south-africa.asp.

6 Ibid.

7 Ibid.

8 Michelle Celarier, "The Mysterious Private Company Controlling Corporate America," *Institutional Investor*, January 29, 2018, https://www.institutionalinvestor.com/article/b16pv9obfozbj8 /the-mysterious-private-company-controlling-corporate-america.

9 Bailard, "FROM SRI TO ESG," 10.

10 Ibid., 10–11.

11 Ibid., 12.

12 Mary Schapiro, "Speech by SEC Chairman: Statement Before the Open Commission Meeting on Disclosure Related to Business or Legislative Events on the Issue of Climate Change," U.S. Securities and Exchange Commission, January 27, 2010, https://www.sec.gov/news/speech/2010/spch012710mls -climate.htm.

13 Bailard, 17.

CHAPTER 7: SETTING THE FIELD

1 Russell Kirk, Review: "Ethical Labor," *The Sewanee Review* 62, no. 3 (Jul.–Sept. 1954): 497.

2 Bower and Paine, "The Error at the Heart," https://hbr.org/2017/05/ managing-for-the-long-term#the-error-at-the-heart-of-corporate-leadership.

3 Chester S. Spatt, "Proxy Advisory Firms, Governance, Failure, and Regulation," Harvard Law School Forum on Corporate Governance, https://corpgov.law.harvard.edu/2019/06/25/proxy-advisory-firms-governance-failure-and -regulation/ (posted June 25, 2019).

4 Nicolas Grabar, Arthur H. Kohn, and David Lopez, "Proxy Advisory Firms— The SEC Drops the Other Shoe," Harvard Law School Forum on Corporate

Governance, posted November 25, 2019. https://corpgov.law.harvard.
edu/2019/11/25/proxy-advisory-firms-the-sec-drops-the-other-shoe/.

5 David A. Bell and Ran Ben-Tzur, "Proxy Voting Guidance Update," Harvard
Law School Forum on Corporate Governance, https://corpgov.law.harvard.
edu/2020/03/05/proxy-voting-guidance-update/ (posted March 5, 2020).

CHAPTER 8: THE PLAYERS, PART ONE: ON THE LEFT

1 David McLaughlin and Annie Massa, "The Hidden Dangers of the Great
Index Fund Takeover," *Bloomberg Businessweek*, January 9, 2020, https://www.
bloomberg.com/news/features/2020-01-09/the-hidden-dangers-of-the-great
-index-fund-takeover.

2 Ibid.

3 Jan Fichtner, Eelke M. Heemskerk, and Javier Garcia-Bernardo, "Hidden power
of the Big Three? Passive index funds, re-concentration of corporate ownership,
and new financial risk," *Business and Politics*, 2017, 306, https://www.cambridge.
org/core/services/aop-cambridge-core/content/view/30AD689509AAD62F5B6
77E916C28C4B6/S1469356917000064a.pdf/hidden_power_of_the_big_three
_passive_index_funds_reconcentration_of_corporate_ownership_and_new
_financial_risk.pdf.

4 Ibid., 307.

5 Larry Fink, "Letter to Shareholders," BlackRock, Inc., https://www.blackrock.
com/corporate/investor-relations/larry-fink-chairmans-letter (posted March
29, 2020).

6 Ryan McMorrow, "BlackRock applies to set up China mutual fund business,"
Financial Times, April 1, 2020, https://www.ft.com/content/fec655ee-1003
-4037-8425-0674615ad832.

7 Hong Kong Exchange (HKEX), "Form 2: Corporate Sustainable Shareholder
Notice," April 17, 2020, https://di.hkex.com.hk/di/NSForm2.aspx?fn=CS202004
17E00041&sa2=ns&sid=1850&sd=17/04/2019&ed=17/04/2020&sa1=cl&scsd=17
/04/2019&sced=17/04/2020&sc=00857&src=Main&lang=EN&tk=ds.

8 Mark L. Melcher and Stephen R. Soukup, "PetroChina Dustup: The Start of
Something Big," Prudential Securities, *Strategy Weekly*, March 22, 2000, https://
www.centerforsecuritypolicy.org/2000/03/30/prudential-securities-potomac
-global-equity-research-perspective-march-22-2000petrochina-dustup-the
-start-of-something-bigby-mark-l-melcher-and-stephen-r-soukup-2/.

9 Free Enterprise Project, "State Street CEO Suggests Company's Leftist
Commitments Are a Promotional Tool," The National Center for Public Policy
Research, May 20, 2020, https://nationalcenter.org/ncppr/2020/05/20/state
-street-ceo-suggests-companys-leftist-commitments-are-a-promotional-ploy/.

10 Ibid.

11 Alex Edmans, *Grow the Pie: How Great Companies Deliver Both Purpose and
Profit* (Cambridge: Cambridge University Press, 2020), 158.

12 Andrew Jones, "ESG firm Domini Impact Investments is to add State Street
Global Advisors as a subadvisor to one of its funds, replacing Wellington
Management Company, *Citywire*, September 7, 2018, https://citywireusa.com/

professional-buyer/news/esg-shop-drops-wellington-for-state-street
-on-800m-fund/a1153083.

13 Domini Funds, "2017 Impact Report," 2018, 26, https://www.domini.com
/uploads/files/reports/Domini_Funds_2017_Impact_Report.pdf.

14 Ibid., 6.

15 Boston Trust Walden, "About," https://www.bostontrustwalden.com/about
-boston-trust-walden/ (accessed August 2, 2020).

16 Influence Watch, "Boston Trust Walden (Walden Asset Management)," Capital
Research Center, https://www.influencewatch.org/for-profit/walden-asset
-management/ (accessed August 2, 2020).

17 Ronald Orol, "Walden to Vanguard: Pushing Exxon on Climate Change Isn't
Enough," *The Street*, July 14, 2017, https://www.thestreet.com/markets/mergers
-and-acquisitions/walden-to-vanguard-pushing-exxon-on-climate-change-isn
-t-enough-14229242.

18 Ray Dalio, "Why and How Capitalism Needs to Be Reformed (Parts 1
& 2)," LinkedIn.com, April 5, 2019, https://www.linkedin.com/pulse/
why-how-capitalism-needs-reformed-parts-1-2-ray-dalio/.

19 American Council for Capital Formation, "ACCF Report: CalPERS and the
Point of No Returns" (press release), December 5, 2017, https://www
.prnewswire.com/news-releases/accf-report-calpers-and-the-point-of-no
-returns-300566788.html.

20 Ibid.

21 Melcher and Soukup, "PetroChina Dustup," https://www
.centerforsecuritypolicy.org/2000/03/30/prudential-securities-potomac-global
-equity-research-perspective-march-22-2000petrochina-dustup-the-start-of
-something-bigby-mark-l-melcher-and-stephen-r-soukup-2/.

22 Jonathan Landay, "U.S. 'looking at' CalPERS holdings in Chinese defense firms:
top White House official," Reuters, March 11, 2020, https://www.reuters
.com/article/us-usa-china-calpers/us-looking-at-calpers-holdings-in-chinese
-defense-firms-top-white-house-official-idUSKBN20Y2GS.

23 Josh Rogin, "For the U.S., the biggest financial threat from China might not be
the coronavirus," *Washington Post*, March 12, 2020, https://www
.washingtonpost.com/opinions/2020/03/12/us-biggest-financial-threat-china
-might-not-be-coronavirus/.

24 Mark J. Perry, "An alarming trend: Managers of public pensions are
increasingly investing funds for their own political agendas," *AEIdeas*, The
American Enterprise Institute, January 12, 2018, https://www.aei.org/carpe
-diem/an-alarming-trend-managers-of-public-pensions-are-increasingly
-investing-funds-for-their-own-political-agendas/.

25 Comptroller, New York City, "MANAGEMENT'S DISCUSSION AND
ANALYSIS (Unaudited)," October 2018, https://comptroller.nyc.gov
/wp-content/uploads/2018/10/Mangement_Discussion_and_Analysis.pdf.

26 Yvan Allaire, "The Troubling Case of Proxy Advisors: Some Policy
Recommendations," Institute for Governance of Private and Public
Organizations, Policy Paper No. 7, January 2013, https://www.sec.gov
/comments/4-725/4725-4549663-176173.pdf.

27 Ibid.

28 Proxy Monitor, "Special Report: Labor-Affiliated Shareholder Activism," The Manhattan Institute, 2014, https://www.proxymonitor.org/Forms/2014Finding3.aspx.

29 Influence Watch, "As You Sow," Capital Research Center, https://www.influencewatch.org/non-profit/as-you-sow/ (accessed August 2, 2020).

30 "2019 SHAREHOLDER ACTION REVIEW: Changing Corporations For Good," As You Sow (asyousow.org), 2019, https://www.asyousow.org/our-work/2019-shareholder-action-review.

31 Heidi Welsh and Michael Passoff, "Proxy Preview 2020," As You Sow (asyousow.org), 2020, https://www.proxypreview.org/2020/report.

32 Ibid.

33 Ibid.

34 Free Enterprise Project, "Free Enterprise Project Blocks Leftist Efforts to Defund Pro-Business Associations," The National Center for Public Policy Research, May 6, 2019, https://nationalcenter.org/ncppr/2019/05/06/free-enterprise-project-blocks-leftist-efforts-to-defund-pro-business-associations/.

35 The Southern Poverty Law Center (SPLCenter.org) "What We Do," https://www.splcenter.org/what-we-do (accessed August 2, 2020).

36 Human Rights Campaign, "HRC Story," https://www.hrc.org/hrc-story (accessed August 2, 2020).

37 Human Rights Campaign, "Annual Reports," https://www.hrc.org/hrc-story/annual-reports (accessed July 16, 2019).

38 Popper, *Conjectures and Refutations*, 124.

39 An Interview with Curtis Ravenel, "How Bloomberg LP has Led the Way in Supporting Material ESG Data," Sustainability Accounting and Standards Board, November 29, 2018, https://www.sasb.org/blog/how-bloomberg-has-lead-the-way-in-supporting-material-esg-data/.

40 "FAF, FASB, and GASB Timeline," Federal Accounting Standards Board, https://www.fasb.org/jsp/FASB/Page/TimelinePage&cid=1175805309640 (accessed August 2, 2020).

41 "Bloomberg SASB ESG Indices," Bloomberg Professional Services, https://www.bloomberg.com/professional/product/indices/sasb/ (accessed August 2, 2020).

42 Ibid.

43 Ian Sherr, "Laurene Powell Jobs invests in news because she worries about democracy," CNET.com, March 1, 2019, https://www.cnet.com/news/laurene-powell-jobs-invests-in-journalism-because-shes-worried-about-democracy/.

44 Todd Spangler, "Laurene Powell Jobs Cuts Disney Stake in Half," *Variety*, February 1, 2017, https://variety.com/2017/digital/news/laurene-powell-jobs-disney-shares-1201975438/.

45 Theodore Schleifer, "Tech billionaires are plotting sweeping, secret plans to boost Joe Biden," *Vox*, May 27, 2020, https://www.vox.com/recode/2020/5/27/21271157/tech-billionaires-joe-biden-reid-hoffman-laurene-powell-jobs-dustin-moskovitz-eric-schmidt.

46 Marc Benioff, "Businesses Are the Greatest Platforms for Change, Huffington Post, January 18, 2016, https://www.huffpost.com/entry/businesses-are-the-greate_b_8993240.

47 Roberto Calasso, *The Ruin of Kasch* (Cambridge: Harvard University Press, 1994), 108.

48 Benioff, "Businesses Are the Greatest Platforms for Change."

49 Marc Benioff, "Marc Benioff: We Need a New Capitalism," *New York Times*, October 14, 2019, https://www.nytimes.com/2019/10/14/opinion/benioff-salesforce-capitalism.html.

50 Ben Hunt, "You Provide the Pictures and I'll Provide the War," Epsilon Theory, September 17, 2018, https://www.epsilontheory.com/you-provide-the-pictures-and-ill-provide-the-war/.

51 Ben Hunt, "But Our Interests Are Aligned!" Epsilon Theory, September 18, 2018, https://www.epsilontheory.com/but-our-interests-are-aligned/.

52 Ibid.

53 Justin Peters, "How Eric Holder Facilitated the Most Unjust Presidential Pardon in American History," *Slate*, July 2, 2013, https://slate.com/news-and-politics/2013/07/marc-rich-presidential-pardon-how-eric-holder-facilitated-the-most-unjust-presidential-pardon-in-american-history.html.

54 Ibid.

55 Matt Taibbi, "Eric Holder, Wall Street Double Agent, Comes in from the Cold," *Rolling Stone*, July 8, 2015, https://www.rollingstone.com/politics/politics-news/eric-holder-wall-street-double-agent-comes-in-from-the-cold-49262/.

56 Eric Holder and Tammy Albarran, "Covington Recommendations," Covington & Burling LLP, 2017, 7, https://drive.google.com/file/d/0B1so8BdVqCgrUVM4UHBpTGROLXM/view.

57 Ibid, 12.

58 Akshaya Kamalnath, "Corporate Diversity 2.0 — Lessons from Silicon Valley's Missteps," *Oregon Review of International Law*, September 25, 2018, https://papers.ssrn.com/sol3/papers.cfm?abstract_id=3254796.

59 SECURITIES AND EXCHANGE COMMISSION, "PROXY DISCLOSURE ENHANCEMENTS (Final Rule)," February 28, 2010, 38–9, https://www.sec.gov/rules/final/2009/33-9089.pdf.

60 "Commonsense Corporate Governance Principles Unveiled by Top Executives," *Business Wire*, January 21, 2016, https://www.businesswire.com/news/home/20160720006555/en/Commonsense-Corporate-Governance-Principles-Unveiled-Top-Executives.

61 Tim Armour et al., "Commonsense Principles 2.0," Commonsense Corporate Governance Principles, July 21, 2016, 1–2, https://www.governanceprinciples.org/wp-content/uploads/2018/10/CommonsensePrinciples2.0.pdf.

62 Larry Fink, "Profit and Purpose," BlackRock, Letter to Clients, 2019, https://www.blackrock.com/americas-offshore/2019-larry-fink-ceo-letter.

63 Charlie Gasparino and Lydia Moynihan, "BlackRock's Larry Fink rattles employees amid political posturing," *FoxBusiness*, January 25, 2019, https://www.foxbusiness.com/business-leaders/blackrocks-larry-fink-rattles-employees-amid-political-posturing.

64 Ibid.

65 Fink, "Profit and Purpose."

66 Bhakti Mirchandani, "The Results Are In: The Surprising Relationship Among Revenue Growth, Board Gender Diversity, and Long-Term Value Creation," *Forbes.com*, March 2, 2020, https://www.forbes.com/sites/bhaktimirchandani /2020/03/02/the-results-are-in-board-gender-diversity-is-as-important-as -revenue-growth-in-long-term-value-creation/#5737c4f64457.

67 Bhakti Mirchandani et al., "Predicting Long-Term Success FOR CORPORATIONS AND INVESTORS WORLDWIDE," FCLT Global, September 29, 2019, https://www.fcltglobal.org/resource /predicting-long-term-success-for-corporations-and-investors-worldwide/.

68 Thomas Maeir, "The Secret Boozy Deals of a Kennedy, a Churchill, and a Roosevelt," *Time*, October 21, 2014, https://time.com/3529756/kennedy -churchill-roosevelt-investment-deal/.

69 *See* 17 C.F.R. § 240.14a-8 (shareholder proposals), *available at* https://www.law .cornell.edu/cfr/text/17/240.14a-8.

70 Ibid.

71 Ibid.

72 Final Rule: Amendments to Rules on Shareholder Proposals, Securities and Exchange Commission, May 21, 1998, https://www.sec.gov/rules/final/34 -40018.htm.

73 *See Staff Legal Bulletin* No. 14J (Oct. 23, 2018), *available at* https://www.sec.gov /corpfin/staff-legal-bulletin-14j-shareholder-proposals.

74 *CorVel Corp.* (issued June 5, 2019) file at 43–5.

75 Ibid., 2.

76 Free Enterprise Institute, "SEC Decisions Raise Specter of Bias, McCarthyism," National Center for Public Policy Research, February 21, 2020, https:// nationalcenter.org/ncppr/2020/02/21/sec-decisions-raise-specter-of-bias -mccarthyism/#12.

77 Ibid.

78 Chartered Financial Analyst Institute, "Board of Governors," https://www. cfainstitute.org/en/about/governance/leadership/board (accessed August 2, 2020).

79 Chartered Financial Analyst Institute, "University Affiliation Program," https:// www.cfainstitute.org/en/about/universities/university-affiliation (accessed August 2, 2020).

80 Chartered Financial Analyst Institute, "Why Hire a CFA Charterholder?" https://www.cfainstitute.org/en/about/employers/hire (accessed August 2, 2020).

81 Chartered Financial Analyst Institute, "ESG Investing and Analysis: What Is ESG Investing?" https://www.cfainstitute.org/en/research/esg-investing (accessed August 2, 2020).

82 Ibid.

83 Chartered Financial Analyst Institute, "Environmental, Social, and Governance (ESG) Working Group," https://www.cfainstitute.org/en/about/governance /committees/esg-working-group (accessed August 2, 2020).

84 Mark Carney, "Resolving the Climate Paradox," speech given at the Arthur Burns Memorial Lecture, Berlin, September 22, 2016, https://www.bankofengland.co.uk/speech/2016/resolving-the-climate-paradox#:~:text=by%20Mark%20Carney-,Resolving%20the%20climate%20paradox%20%2D%20speech%20by%20Mark%20Carney,Arthur%20Burns%20Memorial%20Lecture%2C%20Berlin.&text=The%20Governor%20considers%20the%20financial,could%20help%20resolve%20these%20risks.

85 Glenn D. Rudebusch, "Climate Change and the Federal Reserve," *FRBSF Economic Letter*, March 25, 2019, https://www.frbsf.org/economic-research/publications/economic-letter/2019/march/climate-change-and-federal-reserve/.

86 Ibid.

87 Rusty Guinn, "A New Road to Serfdom," *Epsilon Theory*, January 24, 2020, https://www.epsilontheory.com/a-new-road-to-serfdom/.

88 Ibid.

89 Liz Alderman, "Lagarde Vows to Put Climate Change on the E.C.B.'s Agenda," *New York Times*, September 4, 2019, https://www.nytimes.com/2019/09/04/business/climate-change-ecb-lagarde.html.

90 Patrick Bolton et al., *The Green Swan: Central Banking and Financial Stability in the Age of Climate Change*, The Bank for International Settlements, January, 2020, https://www.bis.org/publ/othp31.pdf.

91 Ibid.

92 "ECB launches public consultation on its guide on climate-related and environmental risks," European Central Bank press release, May 20, 2020, https://www.bankingsupervision.europa.eu/press/pr/date/2020/html/ssm.pr200520~0795c47d73.en.html.

CHAPTER 9: THE PLAYERS, PART TWO: ON THE RIGHT

1 Free Enterprise Project, "About the Free Enterprise Project," National Center for Public Policy Research, https://nationalcenter.org/programs/free-enterprise-project/ (accessed August 2, 2020).

2 Kimberly Strassel, *The Intimidation Game: How the Left is Silencing Free Speech* (New York: Hachette Book Group, 2017).

3 Free Enterprise Project, "Amazon Shareholders Intolerant in the Name of Tolerance," National Center for Public Policy Research, June 25, 2019, https://nationalcenter.org/ncppr/2019/06/25/amazon-shareholders-intolerant-in-the-name-of-tolerance/.

4 American Legislative Exchange Council, "About ALEC," https://www.alec.org/about/#:~:text=The%20American%20Legislative%20Exchange%20Council,government%2C%20free%20markets%20and%20federalism (accessed August 2, 2020).

5 Yvonne Wingett Sanchez and Rob O'Dell, "What is ALEC? 'The most effective organization' for conservatives, says Newt Gingrich," USAToday, April 9, 2019.

6 Strassel, *The Intimidation* Game, 275.

7 Ibid.

8   Robert Armstrong, "Warren Buffett on why companies cannot be moral arbiters," *Financial Times*, December 29, 2019, https://www.ft.com/content /ebbc9b46-1754-11ea-9ee4-11f260415385.

9   Ibid.

10 Ibid.

11 David Sokol et al., CEO Letter to Larry Fink, hosted at ShareholderEquity.org, May 2020, https://shareholderequity.org/campaign/ceos-to-larry-fink/.

CHAPTER 10: THE WORLD'S BIGGEST CORPORATION: ROTTEN TO THE CORE?

1   AppleInsider, June 2020, "Tim Cook addresses George Floyd in employee memo, Apple to donate to human rights groups," https://appleinsider.com /articles/20/06/01/tim-cook-addresses-george-floyd-in-employee-memo-says -apple-to-donate-human-rights-groups.

2   Ibid.

3   Tim Cook, "Tim Cook: Pro-discrimination 'religious freedom' laws are dangerous," *Washington Post*, March 29, 2015, https://www.washingtonpost .com/opinions/pro-discrimination-religious-freedom-laws-are-dangerous-to -america/2015/03/29/bdb4ce9e-d66d-11e4-ba28-f2a685dc7f89_story.html.

4   Aaron K. Chatterji and Michael W. Toffel, "The New CEO Activists," *Harvard Business Review*, January/February 2018, https://hbr.org/2018/01/the-new-ceo -activists.

5   Akane Otani, "Big Technology Stocks Dominate ESG Funds," *Wall Street Journal*, February 11, 2020, https://www.wsj.com/articles/big-technology -stocks-dominate-esg-funds-11581330601.

6   Lila MacLellan, "Apple's Tim Cook has pushed CEO activism into uncharted territory," *Quartz at Work*, October 3, 2019, https://qz.com/work/1721279 /on-daca-apples-tim-cook-pushes-ceo-activism-into-new-territory/.

7   Tim Cook, Twitter, June 11, 2020, https://twitter.com/tim_cook/status /1271113929754685441.

8   Stephen Nellis, "Apple adds Foxconn, chip suppliers to clean energy program," *Reuters*, April 11, 2019, https://www.reuters.com/article/us-apple-energy/apple -adds-foxconn-chip-suppliers-to-clean-energy-program-idUSKCN1RN0JQ?f.

9   Greenpeace International, "Taiwanese suppliers for Apple, HP, Google failing in renewable energy ranking" (press release), May 30, 2019, https://www .greenpeace.org/international/press-release/22139/taiwanese-suppliers-for -apple-hp-google-failing-in-renewable-energy-ranking/.

10 *Ethical Consumer*, "Is Apple Ethical?", https://www.ethicalconsumer.org /company-profile/apple-inc (accessed August 2, 2020).

11 Ibid.

12 Annie Kelly, "Apple and Google named in US lawsuit over Congolese child cobalt mining deaths," *The Guardian*, December 16, 2019, https://www .theguardian.com/global-development/2019/dec/16/apple-and-google-named -in-us-lawsuit-over-congolese-child-cobalt-mining-deaths.

13 Ibid.

14 Brian Merchant, "Life and death in Apple's forbidden city," *The Guardian*, June

18, 2017, https://www.theguardian.com/technology/2017/jun/18/foxconn-life
-death-forbidden-city-longhua-suicide-apple-iphone-brian-merchant-one
-device-extract.

15 David Barboza, "How China Built 'iPhone City' with Billions in Perks for
Apple's Partner," *New York Times*, December 29, 2016, https://www.nytimes.
com/2016/12/29/technology/apple-iphone-china-foxconn.html.

16 Institute on Taxation and Economic Policy, "Fact Sheet: Apple and Tax
Avoidance, November 5, 2017, https://itep.org/fact-sheet-apple-and-tax
-avoidance/#:~:text=The%20major%20strategy%20Apple%20uses,very%20
little%20in%20foreign%20taxes.

17 Rachel King, "Apple's supply chain: A profile of a Foxconn factory employee,"
ZDNet.com, March 29, 2012, https://www.zdnet.com/article/apples-supply
-chain-a-profile-of-a-foxconn-factory-employee/.

18 *Washington Post* Editorial Board, "How China corralled 1 million people
into concentration camps," *Washington Post*, February 9, 2020, https://www.
washingtonpost.com/opinions/global-opinions/a-spreadsheet
-of-those-in-hell-how-china-corralled-uighurs-into-concentration-
camps/2020/02/28/4daeca4a-58c8-11ea-ab68-101ecfec2532_story.html.

CHAPTER 11: IS THE HOUSE OF MOUSE CONTAMINATED BY ROTTEN APPLES?

1 Maureen Dowd, "The Slow-Burning Success of Disney's Bob Iger," *New York
Times*, September 22, 2019, https://www.nytimes.com/2019/09/22/style
/disney-bob-iger-book.html.

2 Maane Khatchatourian, "'Star Wars' China Poster Sparks Controversy After
Shrinking John Boyega's Character," *Variety*, December 4, 2015, https://variety.
com/2015/film/news/star-wars-china-poster-controversy-john-boyega
-1201653494/.

3 Chriss Fuchs, "Tibet Supporters Protest Marvel's 'Doctor Strange' over
Changed Character," *NBC News*, November 3, 2016, https://www.nbcnews
.com/news/asian-america/tibet-supporters-protest-marvel-s-dr-strange-over
-changed-character-n677706.

4 Lisa Richwine, "Disney CEO says it will be 'difficult' to film in Georgia if
abortion law takes effect," *Reuters*, May 29, 2019, https://www.reuters.com
/article/us-usa-abortion-walt-disney-exclusive/exclusive-disney-ceo
-says-it-will-be-difficult-to-film-in-georgia-if-abortion-law-takes-effect
-idUSKCN1T003X.

CHAPTER 12: AMAZON, HATE, AND THE POVERTY PALACE

1 Maria Di Mento, "Jeff Bezos Gives $100 Million to Feeding America's Covid-19
Response Fund," *The Chronicle of Philanthropy*, April 2, 2020, https://www.
philanthropy.com/article/Jeff-Bezos-Gives-100-Million/248416.

2 Paige Leskin, "Here's how much Amazon CEO Jeff Bezos, the richest person
in the world, has personally given to charity," *Business Insider*, March 4, 2020,
https://www.businessinsider.com/jeff-bezos-amazon-how-much-donations
-charity-2019-5#february-2020-10-billion-to-fight-climate-change-through
-the-bezos-earth-fund-11.

3 Jeff Bezos, Instagram, February 17, 2020, https://www.instagram.com/p
/B8rWKFnnQ5c/?utm_source=ig_embed.

4 Fred Lucas, "Conservatives Ask Amazon to End SPLC's Role as 'Hate
Group' Sheriff," *The Daily Signal*, May 21, 2020, https://www.dailysignal.
com/2020/05/21/conservatives-ask-amazon-to-end-splcs-role-as-hate-group
-sheriff/.

5 Kyle Smith, "Hate, Inc.: The SPLC Is a Hyper-Partisan Scam," *National Review
Online*, March 1, 2018, https://www.nationalreview.com/2018/03/southern
-poverty-law-center-bias-hate-group-labels-scam/.

6 Ibid.

7 Tyler O'Neil, "Exaggerating Hate Pays: Scandal-Plagued SPLC Has Millions in
Offshore Accounts, Half a Billion in Assets," *PJMedia*, April 29, 2020, https://
pjmedia.com/news-and-politics/tyler-o-neil/2020/04/29/exaggerating
-hate-pays-scandal-plagued-splc-has-162m-in-offshore-accounts-500m-in
-assets-n386741.

8 Tyler O'Neil, "The SPLC's Scandalous History on Race," *PJMedia*, March 20,
2019, https://pjmedia.com/news-and-politics/tyler-o-neil/2019/03/20/the-splcs
-scandalous-history-on-race-n64496.

9 Bob Moser, "The Reckoning of Morris Dees and the Southern Poverty Law
Center," *The New Yorker*, March 21, 2019, https://www.newyorker.com/news
/news-desk/the-reckoning-of-morris-dees-and-the-southern-poverty-law
-center.

10 Nathan J. Robinson, "The Southern Poverty Law Center Is Everything That's
Wrong With Liberalism," *Current Affairs*, March 26, 2019, https://www.
currentaffairs.org/2019/03/the-southern-poverty-law-center-is-everything
-thats-wrong-with-liberalism.

11 Ibid.

12 Ibid.

13 David Nussman, "SPLC Gets Catholics Removed from Amazon Smile,"
ChurchMilitant.com, April 25, 2018, https://www.churchmilitant.com/news
/article/catholics-turned-away-from-amazon-smile.

14 Tyler O'Neil, "Shareholders Pressure Amazon to Drop Corrupt Leftist Group
Behind 'Viewpoint Discrimination,'" *PJMedia*, May 12, 2020, https://pjmedia.
com/culture/tyler-o-neil/2020/05/12/shareholders-pressure-amazon-to-drop
-corrupt-leftist-group-behind-viewpoint-discrimination-n390236.

15 Bruce Haring, "Amazon CEO Jeff Bezos Explains His Company's BLM Support
in Response to Customer Complaint," Deadline.com, June 5, 2020, https://
deadline.com/2020/06/jeff-bezos-underlines-amazon-blm-support-instagram
-post-1202952597/.

16 Tyler O'Neil, "Report Shows Online Ties Linking HuffPost, the Guardian, and
SPLC to Antifa," *PJMedia*, May 21, 2019, https://pjmedia.com/news-and
-politics/tyler-o-neil/2019/05/21/report-shows-online-ties-linking-huffpost
-the-guardian-and-splc-to-antifa-n65988.

17 Charlie Wood, "Longtime Amazon VP Tim Bray just quit in dismay, calling
the company 'chickens---' for firing workers who criticized it," *Business Insider*,

May 4, 2020, https://www.businessinsider.com/amazon-engineer-resigned-treatment-warehouse-whistleblowers-2020-5?r=US&IR=T.

18 Jason Del Rey, "Amazon's top spokesperson walks back controversial comments for the second time in a month," *Vox*, October 31, 2019, https://www.vox.com/recode/2019/10/31/20941247/amazon-jay-carney-spokesperson-world-series-umpires-tweet-apology.

INDEX